*This book is for educational purposes. Individual results will vary. The author makes no guarantees of income or business success. References to specific software tools reflect the author's personal experience and opinions at the time of writing. Tool pricing, features, and availability may change — always verify current information directly with the vendors. Always consult appropriate professionals before making significant business or financial decisions. Some prompts in this book are designed to generate persuasive copy — use them ethically and honestly in your own business.*

Published by MMS Vegas. First edition.

ISBN: 979-8-9961264-0-8 (paperback)
ISBN: 979-8-9961264-1-5 (ebook)

*For everyone who ever looked at a marketing agency invoice and thought: there has to be a better way. There is.*

# A Letter From the Author: How I Went From Needing A Full Team of Specialists To Being A Force Of One

---

Dear Reader,

I want to tell you something up front so you know what kind of book this is. I built everything you're about to learn — the funnels, the automations, the copy, the strategy — without hiring a single developer, designer, or copywriter.

That wasn't always the case.

For the first forty years of my career, I was completely dependent on other people. Need a website? Call the web designer and wait three weeks. Landing page idea? Hire a developer and blow half your budget before you even know if the idea works. Need graphics for an ad campaign? Find an artist, explain the vision, get back something that's sixty percent of what you wanted, then sit through three rounds of revisions.

I was a marketing guy hamstrung by the technical skills I didn't have.

I'm officially retired now. But here's the thing about entrepreneurs — we never really stop. I still get excited about new projects, new ideas, and challenging problems to chew on. Every project needs marketing — the difference is today I don't need to wait on anyone else to execute the vision in my head.

In the old world, every project was a Gantt chart of sourcing talent, explaining requirements, waiting for deliverables, and hoping what came back matched what I was picturing. By the time the work was done, I'd spent weeks and thousands of dollars (often my own) just to test an idea that might not even work.

What I've discovered over the past two years is that the AI tools available to everyone are absolutely mind-blowing! With the right AI tools and the right prompts, I can research markets, develop strategies, write sales copy, build landing pages and funnels, design graphics, create automations, and optimize the whole thing for performance — all in the time it used to take me to write a project brief for my client.

I'm not saying you'll never need experts again. If you're designing the next Tesla or building a mission-critical enterprise platform, you're still going to need specialists, but for ninety percent of what most businesses need to succeed online — the stuff that actually moves the needle — you can now do it yourself, faster than you could outsource it, and for the price of a few monthly software subscriptions.

None of this is theory — I quite literally use the systems in this book every day, running a real business that generates real revenue with no team and no agency. The funnels and prompts in these chapters are the same ones I run for myself and that's exactly what this book is going to do for you.

You're not going to become a programmer. You're going to bend AI to your will and get programming done without any programmers. Same principle applies to copy, design, email strategy, and everything else in the stack. You're more of a "general contractor" letting AI do most of the specialist work at your direction. I tried to explain it to my mother and told her to think of it like when the pilot on the airplane has a heart attack and a passenger has to get in the cockpit with air traffic control and land the plane. He's not a trained pilot, but with someone guiding his every move he can execute the necessary steps to often get the plane on the ground safely. It's much the same way if you watch me "coding" with Claude.

The tools exist and the methods work. The only real question is whether you're willing to do the work of learning how to use them properly — which is most of what the rest of this book is about. I've provided lots of canned prompts to get you started, but once you become more comfortable you'll develop your own style and unique way of prompting that suits you.

Let's get started.

— Brian

P.S. Everything in this book has been tested in real businesses generating real revenue. This isn't academic theory, and it isn't aspirational. It's a field guide written by someone who's spent the last two years in the weeds making every one of these systems work. If you've got more vision than budget, you're in the right place.

## Introduction: The $14,400 Wake-Up Call

---

The invoice arrived on a Tuesday.

My client had hired a marketing agency — a real one, with a downtown office and a guy named Chad who wore slim-fit blazers and carried a MacBook like it was a religious artifact — to build out a product line's digital presence. They'd been working for about six weeks. I was on a separate project at the time, but I'd chat them up by the coffee machine. The invoice was specific about the total: $14,400.

The deliverables: a logo they didn't love, a strategy document full of important-sounding words that didn't contain a lot of actionable data, and a landing page that converted at 1.2 percent. For those who don't know what that means: for every hundred people who visited it, ninety-nine looked at it and left. Chad charged my client fourteen thousand dollars to build a page that worked one time in a hundred, and I thought to myself, there has to be a better way.

There is. And it costs less than a few bucks a day.

This is not an AI book. It's a direct-response and business strategy guide turbo-charged by AI. The tools are new but the principles behind them are timeless.

## The One-Person Marketing Department

You are now the marketing department. Claude is your research team, your strategist, and your copywriter. The funnel software is the wireframe of your marketing and automation plan. One human with software and AI all available on a student budget.

That's the central idea of this book. Every framework, every prompt, every sequence that follows exists to build and operate that model. The goal is not to replace thinking, but to increase what one person can do with the same number of hours. Less time executing, more time thinking.

A marketing agency charges $50,000 to build this infrastructure for you. This book costs $9.99. The difference is that you can now run the department yourself (which, after decades of watching businesses pay agencies for work they could have done better with the right system) strikes me as a reasonable trade.

## My Background, and Why It Matters for You

I want to be upfront about where I'm coming from, because context matters when you're deciding whether to trust someone's advice.

I've spent forty years in direct response advertising. Not brand advertising, not the kind designed to make you feel good about a company, but the kind measured in dollars in and dollars out. In my opinion there's no truer measure of successful advertising.

It's the kind where you write the ad, you run the ad, and the phone rings or it doesn't. You know within days whether your copy worked. There's nowhere to hide in direct response.

Over four decades, I've sold cell phones, satellite television, merchandise, financial products, and a dozen other categories. The campaigns I've been involved with have generated hundreds of millions of dollars in measurable, trackable sales. I've written or overseen copy for every format direct response has operated in: television, radio, print, direct mail, and eventually digital.

The principles that make marketing work have not changed in forty years. People still respond to clear promises, specific benefits, honest proof, and a well-constructed reason to act now rather than later. What has changed, radically, in the last several years is how accessible those principles have become to someone who isn't a forty-year veteran. AI tools have done something extraordinary: they've made strategic, well-crafted direct response marketing accessible to anyone willing to learn how to use them properly.

When I started using Claude for marketing work, I wasn't looking for a novelty. I was testing whether it could deliver on the principles I'd spent a career mastering at a professional level. The answer (with the right approach) is yes. This book is my attempt to give you that approach without the forty-year learning curve.

## A Note on Tools: Any AI, Any Funnel Software

Throughout this book, I use Claude from Anthropic as the AI of choice and FunnelKit Pro as the funnel-building tool. All the prompts are written for Claude. All the funnel build references point to FunnelKit Pro.

Claude is an AI assistant created by Anthropic that excels at complex reasoning, analysis, and writing tasks. Unlike simple chatbots, Claude understands context, applies strategic frameworks, and produces sophisticated marketing copy that rivals human professionals.

I want to be clear upfront: you can apply every principle and every framework in this book using any capable AI assistant and any reputable funnel software. ChatGPT, Gemini, or any other large language model will respond to these prompts with comparable results. ClickFunnels, Kartra, GoHighLevel, Systeme.io, or any other funnel platform can implement the same sequences and flows I describe.

My preference for Claude is based on its performance on nuanced writing and strategic reasoning tasks. My preference for FunnelKit Pro is based on cost, data ownership, and the fact that it runs on your own WordPress site rather than a third-party platform. Those are my informed opinions after extensive use, not the only valid choices.

If you're already using a different AI or a different funnel platform, don't switch just for this book. Learn the principles here, adapt the prompts to your tool, and apply the frameworks with whatever software you have. The system works across platforms.

## What to Expect

This is a system book, not a theory book. Every chapter answers a specific operational question. Every prompt is a tool you use immediately. Your individual results will depend on market selection, offer quality, and execution — the same variables they've always depended on. What changes is how fast and how cheaply you can act on your instinct and good judgment, which is ultimately what this book is about teaching you to do.

## How to Use This Book

Read it in order the first time. The parts build on each other. When you reach a Prompt Box, open your AI tool and run it. Reading prompts is about ten percent as useful as using them. After the first read, keep the book as a reference. Every time you build something new, come back and re-run the relevant prompts with fresh context.

**POWER TIP:** Claude has skills and project memory that save you endless repetitive prompting. Load your business context, brand voice guidelines, and strategic frameworks into Claude once, and ask it to reference them before completing whatever task you're giving it. This becomes even less time-consuming as you become confident with the tools.

## The System in Action: A 60-Day Transformation

---

*Before the marketing wireframes and the AI prompts, here is a concrete demonstration of what the system in this book can produce — a composite example drawn from real funnel implementations across similar direct-to-consumer brands. The design, the sequence, and the numbers reflect what you can expect with this approach when properly executed.*

### Flagship Case Study: 60-Day Transformation

**Small-Batch Hot Sauce Brand**

### The Situation

A small-batch artisan hot sauce brand was generating roughly $3,200 a month in revenue, almost entirely from returning customers and market regulars. Average order value was $18. The founder had a product people loved but no system for consistently converting new customers. Cold traffic to the product page wasn't converting. The brand's story of small-batch production, real ingredients, and a specific culinary philosophy was compelling but not being communicated. Visitors landed on a product listing and then left.

### How the System Was Used

The first Claude session focused entirely on the customer avatar: who specifically was the ideal first-time buyer, what did they already believe about hot sauce, what frustrated them about commercial brands, and what did they say when they recommended a favorite product to a friend. From that session came the copy direction for every page in the funnel. Not generic "premium artisan" language, but specific claims grounded in what customers actually said.

The free-plus-shipping offer was redesigned around a single sampler bottle at no cost, with shipping covered. The checkout page added an order bump: a digital "Sauce Notes" guide containing recipes, pairing suggestions, and heat management techniques, written in one afternoon with Claude and priced at $9. A one-click upsell offered a three-bottle mixed variety pack at $54. The post-purchase email sequence, six emails over thirty days, educated, entertained, and introduced the full product range.

## Results — 60 Days

Average order value increased from $18 to $34 within sixty days of the funnel launching, driven by an upsell take rate of approximately 22 percent and an order bump take rate of approximately 31 percent. Monthly revenue climbed to approximately $7,800 over the following six months as the owner incrementally increased ad spend with confidence in the funnel economics.

## Key Lesson

Growth did not come from more traffic. Rather, it came from maximizing the revenue of each customer. Once you've done that, scale becomes affordable, predictable, and profitable. The digital order bump was a PDF guide that cost nothing to produce and nothing to fulfill, and it became the highest-margin product in the lineup. Using Claude made it fast and easy to write — something that would have been outsourced to an outside pro adding additional time and money to the budget.

# Part One: The New Playing Field

---

# Chapter 1: Why Now — What Changed in the Last Two Years

---

Ten years ago, if you wanted to build a serious online business from scratch — something more than an Etsy shop or a hobby project, a real revenue-generating business — you needed to either spend years acquiring expertise or spend money on people who already had it. The copywriter who could write a converting sales page charged $3,000 to $8,000. The funnel consultant charged $5,000 just to tell you what to build. The developer charged $150 an hour to build it.

The total cost of taking an idea from concept to functional marketing infrastructure, done properly, was somewhere between $30,000 and $100,000. For a bootstrapped operator, that was an insurmountable barrier.

Two things happened simultaneously that restructured those economics. AI tools reached genuine capability for marketing and strategy work, not surface-level familiarity but deep, usable expertise you can access without specialized training and direct toward your specific situation. The tools for building marketing infrastructure matured to the point where a solo operator can build copy, landing pages, sales funnels, marketing automations, and complete market research — work that previously required an entire development team and now happens in a fraction of the time.

## What Changed

The first change was AI, specifically, the emergence of large language models like Claude that have genuine, broad-based expertise in marketing, strategy, psychology, and business development. Not surface-level familiarity — deep, usable knowledge that you can access conversationally and direct toward your exact scenario.

The knowledge that used to live exclusively in the heads of expensive specialists now lives in a system you can access for about twenty dollars a month. That isn't a small thing, it's a radical redistribution of expertise at a scale that has no real precedent.

The second big change was the development of no-code/low-code tools for building marketing infrastructure — FunnelKit Pro lets a solo operator build checkout flows, upsell sequences, and marketing automations that would have required a development team and a significant budget just a decade ago. The technical barrier is really non-existent now.

Both changes happened around the same time, and the combination is what makes this opportunity extraordinary. Strategy and execution were both gated behind money and expertise and now both are available to anyone willing to learn how to use them.

## How Much Money Are We Talking About?

Here are some before and after numbers for you to consider.

Market research from a traditional firm: $8,000 to $25,000, four to eight weeks and you have a PDF report that's already dated by the time you read it. With a capable AI tool, the research approach described in Part Two and a few hours, you can have, at a fraction of the cost output specifically tailored to your questions and not a generic industry report.

A complete funnel with copy, including the landing page, checkout, email sequence, and upsell pages, written by a freelance copywriter: $3,000 to $10,000, two to four weeks. With AI and the prompting approach in Part Seven you'll have a working first draft in hours. Editing to final takes longer, but editing is dramatically faster than writing from scratch.

Funnel software on a third-party platform like ClickFunnels: $97 to $297 per month, every month, on infrastructure you don't own. FunnelKit Pro running on your own WordPress site: under $30 per month annualized, on a platform you control. (Both figures reflect 2026 pricing; software pricing changes, so verify current rates with each vendor.)

The point isn't that AI and modern software make everything free. They don't. The point is that the gap between what a well-resourced business can build and what a solo operator can build has narrowed dramatically. The tools available today change the economics of building something real, and the playing field is wide open for the solo player and small team to compete at the highest levels.

## The Competitive Advantage of Moving Now

Early adopters gain advantages that are real but not permanent — the people who learned search engine optimization effectively in 2005 had advantages over those who learned in 2015. The same was true with people building email lists in 2010 having advantages over those who started in 2020. The tools didn't stop working but the baseline shifted.

The same dynamic is playing out with AI-augmented marketing right now. Operators who develop genuine skill with these tools will earn advantages that get harder to close as the tools become more widely adopted. There will be a widening gap between skilled operators and average ones, and the gap is forming now.

There's no deadline — only the compounding advantage of developing real capability earlier rather than later.

## What This Looks Like: A Concrete Example

Let me give you a concrete picture of what this workflow looks like in practice.

Consider a business selling specialty food products online: hand-crafted hot sauces, small-batch preserves, artisan jerky. Businesses like this often operate on a limited-release model where specific products are available for a short window, in limited quantities, with an email list as the primary sales channel. The emotional mechanics involved are similar to a sneaker drop: scarcity, craft provenance, collector identity, community belonging.

Before an AI-augmented workflow, launching a new product looked like this for most small food producers: several weeks of writing and rewriting product descriptions, three or four drafts of a launch email sequence, a product page they'd agonize over for days, and a lot of time spent wondering if any of it was good enough. The cycle from "I want to release this" to "it's ready to launch" was often six to eight weeks.

With the workflow in this book, that same cycle compresses to a week or ten days. You and Claude work as a one-person team that can quickly organize the story around a specific product, including the origin, the ingredients, what makes it different, who made it, and why. Brainstorm with Claude to workshop the offer structure and check pricing logic against your customer avatar, then use it to draft the email sequence and refine it in your voice. Finally, use it to identify the emotional angle for the product page.

The outputs aren't perfect out of the box. Everything needs editing, because your voice is specific and the AI is working from your instructions rather than years of your history. But the edited versions are consistently better than what most solo operators produce on their own, and they're done in a fraction of the time.

More importantly, you're doing all the work that usually gets skipped, the strategic work, market intelligence work, the competitive positioning analysis, and the customer avatar refinement. Most small business owners know they should be doing these things but never have the bandwidth when they're also trying to keep all the other balls up in the air. With AI handling more of the execution, you have more capacity for the strategic thinking that moves the business.

That's a real value proposition, not just faster outputs, but the capacity shift that lets you do the work you were skipping.

## The Honest Caveat

I've said some enthusiastic things about Claude in this chapter, and I want to balance them with an honest caveat before we go further.

Claude is not magic. It's a capable tool that amplifies your thinking. If your thinking is unclear, it will amplify unclear thinking into more words. If your strategic inputs are vague, it will produce vague outputs at greater length. The quality of what you get out is fundamentally constrained by the quality of what you put in.

That's why a big portion of this book is devoted to prompting. Not just giving you prompts to copy, but teaching you the principles behind effective prompting so you can write your own. The difference between a mediocre Claude output and an excellent one is rarely about Claude's capability. It's about the specificity, context, and strategic framing of the prompt.

I've seen people try to use AI as a substitute for understanding their market and their customer. They skip the research, prompt Claude for a customer avatar, and treat the output as real knowledge, but it isn't. Claude synthesizes broad information, but it doesn't know your specific customers, your specific community, or the specific nuances of your niche. Those things require a real, knowledgeable operator — you. Claude can help you organize and act on that knowledge but it can't replace the need to acquire it.

Keep that caveat in mind as you work through the book. Use Claude to accelerate and enhance your thinking, not to substitute for it.

# Chapter 2: Your $50,000 Marketing Team Is Now Available for $90 a Month

---

Before we do anything practical, I want to give you a mental model for working with Claude — because the mental model is what separates people who get real value out of it from people who decide after a week that it's overhyped.

The most common mistake people make with Claude is treating it like a search engine. They type a question, read the answer, then move on. That works for simple factual queries but for planning marketing it's really missing the mark.

Think of Claude as a brilliant, broadly educated business partner who has read everything, charges you less than a streaming subscription, works at any hour, and has no ego about being told it's wrong. It's not a specialist in your niche, it has never run a business of its own, and it doesn't know the specific history of your market, the lingo of your community, or the way your specific customers talk. But it is exceptionally good at applying frameworks, synthesizing information, generating options, and helping you think through problems from angles you hadn't considered and you can go a long way towards teaching Claude all of these things over time.

That combination — broad expertise, zero ego, infinite patience, genuine willingness to collaborate — is what makes Claude so useful for business work. You are not delegating to Claude, you are collaborating with Claude and the quality of what you get out depends on what you put in.

### What Claude Is Actually Good At

Synthesis is where Claude does its best work. Bring it a pile of raw material — competitor reviews, forum posts, customer interviews, your own scattered notes — and ask it to find the patterns. It will surface themes you missed, spot contradictions, and organize the chaos into something you can actually act on. What used to require a research analyst at $200 an hour and a week of turnaround now takes an afternoon.

Then there's option generation. When you're stuck between three positioning angles, ask for ten more. When you need a headline, ask for fifteen variations and pick the two strongest. When you're trying to figure out the right order bump for your checkout page, have Claude generate twelve candidates ranked by how well they complement the core offer. The real value here is that you stop getting protective about your first idea. The first idea is almost never the best one.

You'll find that there are innumerable ways to answer a question and to consistently get answers close to what you're looking for. Learning to properly frame your prompts is the skill most people underestimate. Tell Claude to run your pricing decision through the Three-Lever Framework, to analyze your positioning through Porter's Five Forces, or to do a Jobs-to-be-Done analysis on why a customer would choose you over a direct competitor, and it will apply those frameworks rigorously and specifically. This is where the prompts in this book earn their keep. The frameworks are baked into the prompts, so you get strategically sophisticated outputs even if you've never read the original books the frameworks came from.

First drafts are where the real time savings show up. Not final drafts — the voice almost always needs editing, and Claude sometimes drifts toward a more formal register than any of us want. But as a way of getting past the blank page, and getting something on screen that you can react to, Claude consistently produces drafts that are faster to edit than they would have been to write from scratch.

Give Claude specific feedback on what worked and what didn't, and it adjusts on the next pass. Humans do this too, but humans get tired and humans get defensive about choices they've already made. Claude has no attachment to what it wrote thirty seconds ago. It will revise the same piece eight times if the piece needs it, and it's just as engaged on the eighth draft as it was on the first.

## What Claude Is Not Good At

Just as important to be honest about the limitations, because the people who get frustrated with Claude are almost always asking it to do things it genuinely can't do.

Feed it current data. Claude's knowledge base has a cutoff date, and after that date it doesn't know what's happened. It doesn't know what your competitors launched last week, what Facebook's current CPM rates are, or whether a specific software tool still exists in its current form. For anything time-sensitive you either bring the information to the session yourself or you use a version of Claude with live web search turned on — which helps, but isn't the same as a human expert with their finger on the pulse of your specific market.

Long, sprawling sessions are where the second limitation shows up. When a conversation covers too many topics over too many hours, Claude loses the thread. It forgets a decision you made at the start. It drifts back into assumptions you explicitly ruled out. The fix is boring but effective: keep a context document, paste it at the start of important sessions, and remind Claude of the key constraints when the conversation stretches. We'll come back to this later in the book.

Direct customer knowledge is the third gap, and I encourage you not to underestimate its importance. Claude generates sophisticated hypotheses about what your customers want, but it has never met your customers — it doesn't know the specific language your community uses, the specific fears of your specific buyer, or the shared references that would make your copy feel written from the inside. That knowledge only comes from real contact — forums, interviews, reviews, conversations — and no amount of AI synthesis substitutes for the work of gathering it. Claude helps you organize and act on customer knowledge, but it can't hand it to you.

Another honest caveat every serious Claude user eventually learns: it is occasionally wrong about specific facts, with the kind of confidence that can mislead you if you're not paying attention. This happens more with statistics, numbers, and dates than with strategic reasoning — but it happens. Verify anything specific before you publish it.

### Setting Up For Business Work

You access Claude at claude.ai. The free account gets you started. The paid plan — Claude Pro, about $20 a month at the time of writing — removes the rate limits and gives you access to the most capable model. For the level of work this book describes, the paid plan is worth it. The free-tier rate limits will hit you at the worst possible moment, usually right when you're on a roll.

The single habit that produces more value than any other setup step is writing a context document for every business you work on. A plain text file, nothing fancy, containing the things Claude would need to know to be useful. What you sell. Who your customer is. How you talk about yourself. Your pricing. Your key differentiators. The decisions you've already made and don't want to re-litigate. At the start of every significant session, you paste this document in before you type your first prompt.

The difference between a cold prompt and a contextualized one is dramatic. Claude works with what you give it. Give it everything relevant and you get outputs grounded in your actual business. Give it nothing and you get generic outputs that could apply to anyone selling anything.

Here's a template for a basic business context document:

**✦ BUSINESS CONTEXT DOCUMENT TEMPLATE**

```
BUSINESS CONTEXT – [YOUR BUSINESS NAME]
WHAT WE SELL: [Clear description of your product or service]
WHO WE SELL TO: [Your customer avatar – be specific: not
'health-conscious adults' but 'women aged 32-48 who have
tried every diet and are finally open to a different
approach']
CORE PAIN WE SOLVE: [The one thing that drives people to us]
OUR POSITIONING: [How we're different from alternatives]
PRICE POINTS: [Your key products and their prices]
BRAND VOICE: [How we write and talk – conversational vs
formal, profanity or not, specific phrases we use, things we
never say]
DECISIONS ALREADY MADE: [Things you don't want Claude
suggesting you change or revisit]
CURRENT PROJECT: [What we're working on right now]
CONSTRAINTS: [Budget, timeline, technical limitations,
anything else Claude should know]
```

**Note:** *Build a version of this for your business now, before you go further in the book. Even if some fields are incomplete, it's worth having. Update it as your thinking develops. I have a version of this for every business project I'm running.*

## The Collaboration Rhythm

When I'm using Claude for serious business work, the session has a rhythm. I paste the context document. I make one specific request — not a list of things I want, one thing. I read the output carefully. I identify what's right, what's wrong, and what's missing. I give specific feedback. I read the revised output. Then it's just wash, rinse, and repeat until it's good enough to use.

This sounds like a lot of steps for something that's supposed to be fast. In practice, the whole cycle for a piece of copy — first prompt to usable draft — takes fifteen to twenty minutes. Market research synthesis, forty-five minutes to an hour. A full offer design, a couple of hours spread across a few sessions. That is dramatically faster than any previous alternative. It just requires you to stay engaged instead of hoping the first output is magically perfect.

The single biggest upgrade you can make to your prompting is learning to give feedback at the sentence level. Don't say "make this better." Say: "The second paragraph loses energy — cut it to two sentences. The third paragraph uses the word 'optimize' which sounds corporate — replace it with something conversational. The CTA at the end is weak — make it more specific and direct." That kind of feedback produces dramatic improvement on the next pass, because now Claude knows exactly what to change and what to leave alone.

Think of it as directing rather than generating. You're the director. Claude is the writer in the chair. Good directors give specific notes. They don't say "be better" and walk away.

## Chapter 3: The 3-Tool Stack That Replaces a $100,000 Agency

---

One of the most reliably expensive traps in online business is software accumulation. It starts with one tool you need. Then you discover a tool that solves a specific problem with that tool. Then you need something to connect those two tools. Then someone recommends something else. Before long, you're paying $400 a month in software subscriptions for tools that overlap, underdeliver, and don't talk to each other.

I've been there. Most people building online businesses have been there. The antidote is deliberately building the minimal viable stack, the smallest set of tools that covers your actual needs, and resisting the pull to add complexity until you have a specific, named reason that existing tools can't address.

Here's the stack I use and recommend. It covers everything you need to research markets, build funnels, run automations, manage email marketing, and process payments. It doesn't cover everything every online business will ever need, but it covers the core infrastructure for ninety percent of businesses at the stage this book is aimed at.

### The Foundation: WordPress and WooCommerce

Let me preface this section by first saying you don't have to understand what any of the following tools are or how they work, once you decide what your stack looks like Claude can help any level operator set it all up. WordPress is the foundation. It runs approximately 43 percent of all websites globally, it's free, and it's the most extensible platform available. You could spend years learning everything about WordPress and never run out of things to learn, but you don't need to. For our purposes, you need to know how to set up pages, install plugins, and navigate the admin dashboard. That's it.

WooCommerce is the e-commerce layer that goes on top of WordPress. Also free. It turns your WordPress site into a functional store that handles products, inventory, payments, orders, and customers. If you're selling physical products, digital downloads, services, or subscriptions, WooCommerce handles the transaction mechanics.

For hosting, I use SiteGround. Specifically the GoGeek plan, which gives you the resources and technical features you need to run a serious business site without paying enterprise prices. Around $200 to $250 per year, which works out to about $20 a month. Do not buy the cheapest hosting available. Slow hosting costs you conversions, real and measurable, and the money saved is a false economy.

For your theme, the visual layer that controls what your site looks like, I use Flatsome, which costs about $59 as a one-time purchase on ThemeForest. Elementor (the free version) handles most page-building needs on top of Flatsome. There are other good options; these are the ones I know work well together.

### The Marketing Layer: FunnelKit Pro

FunnelKit Pro is the tool that transforms a standard WordPress/WooCommerce site into a genuine marketing machine. It has two main components: FunnelKit Funnel Builder and FunnelKit Automations.

Funnel Builder handles the pages and the flow. It gives you conversion-optimized checkout pages, the ability to add order bumps to checkout, one-click upsells that fire after payment without requiring customers to re-enter payment information, A/B testing built into the funnel builder, and all the page-building functionality you need for landing pages, thank you pages, and sales pages.

FunnelKit Automations is the marketing automation engine. It handles the marketing sequences that fire based on what customers do: welcome sequences when someone joins your list, cart abandonment sequences when someone doesn't complete checkout, post-purchase sequences that build the relationship after a sale, and milestone sequences that trigger at specific behavior thresholds.

The pricing comparison alone makes a compelling case. ClickFunnels, the most heavily marketed alternative, charges $97 to $297 per month. Kartra charges $119 to $549 per month. Kajabi starts at $149 per month. FunnelKit Pro runs $99 to $249 per year. Not per month. Per year. For a business you're going to run for years, that difference is thousands of dollars in recovered operating costs.

Honestly, the cost isn't even the main argument. The main argument is that FunnelKit runs on your site, which means your customer data stays in your system, your products live in WooCommerce where everything else is integrated, and you're not dependent on a third-party platform’s uptime, pricing decisions, or feature roadmap. You own the infrastructure.

For the official technical documentation, see funnelkit.com. For the operator's playbook — how to actually use FunnelKit to run a store, with the worked examples and production patterns the documentation doesn't cover — see The Missing Manual for FunnelKit, also published by MMS Vegas. In this book, I give you enough context to understand what's possible and why it matters.

## The Email Layer

You need an email marketing platform separate from FunnelKit. FunnelKit handles automation sequences triggered by user behavior. Your email platform handles transmitting your emails (the ones you write and send to your whole list) and often serves as the list management system that stores subscriber data.

For most businesses starting out, Mailchimp works and is free up to a certain list size (I use Mailmunch). It integrates cleanly with WordPress and handles both list building (opt-in forms, pop-ups) and drip sequences. ActiveCampaign is more powerful and more expensive, worth it when you’re at a scale that needs the sophistication.

Make sure your email platform connects to FunnelKit so that funnel events (opt-ins, purchases, abandoned carts) can trigger your email sequences automatically. All the major platforms have integrations for this.

### The Intelligence Layer: Claude

Claude Pro: twenty dollars a month. This is your research department, your strategist, your copywriter, your offer consultant, and your marketing brain trust. Relative to what these functions cost when you hire humans, it is almost comically affordable.

Get the Pro plan. The free tier is fine for occasional use. For the workflow described in this book, with its regular sessions, long outputs, and multiple iterations, you'll hit the rate limits at the worst possible moments.

### The Full Stack, In Summary

WordPress + WooCommerce (free) + SiteGround GoGeek hosting (~$20/month) + Flatsome theme ($59 one-time) + Elementor free + FunnelKit Pro (~$15–20/month when annualized) + email platform (free to ~$30/month depending on list size) + Claude Pro ($20/month). Total monthly cost: approximately $55 to $90 depending on the email platform you choose and your list size.

That's your complete marketing and sales infrastructure. Compare that to: ClickFunnels Basic ($97/month) + Kajabi ($149/month) + a copywriter

($500+ per project) + a market researcher (per project) + Claude ($20/month) = $300+ per month plus per-project costs, on platforms you don't own.

The stack I've described gets you everything the expensive stack gets you for a fraction of the cost on infrastructure you control.

One more note: resist the urge to add tools. The more tools you add, the more time you spend managing tools instead of building your business. Add something only when you have a specific, current problem that the existing stack can't solve, and not before you've exhausted what you can do with what you already have.

### A Note on Pricing

Every dollar figure cited in this chapter was accurate at the time of writing. Software pricing changes. Sometimes up, sometimes down, sometimes the product disappears entirely. Before you spend a dollar on any tool mentioned here, verify current pricing directly with the vendor. The stack I've described has been stable for years, but don't take my word for current numbers.

# Part Two: Research and Market Selection

# Chapter 4: Market Research in an Afternoon, Not a Month

---

Most businesses fail at one specific thing: market selection. Execution wasn't the problem. The product wasn't the problem. Marketing wasn't the problem. They picked the wrong market. Someone builds a good product, writes decent copy, builds a reasonably functional funnel, and drives traffic to it, and nothing much happens. Because the market was too small, or too competitive, or the customers weren't in enough pain to spend money solving the problem, or the customers who were in pain couldn't be reached efficiently.

Market selection is the strategic decision everything else is built on. Get it right and everything downstream is easier. Get it wrong and you're pushing a boulder uphill indefinitely.

The good news: the tools we have now make market selection faster and more rigorous than it has ever been. A day of careful research and Claude-assisted synthesis will give you more market intelligence than most businesses operate on indefinitely.

## The Three Criteria That Matter

I've evaluated dozens of market opportunities over the years and simplified my evaluation down to three questions. If you can answer yes to all three, you have something worth investigating further. If you can't, stop and find a different opportunity before you invest significant time and money.

**Question one: Are there people in this market who are in real pain?** Not mild inconvenience. Not moderate discomfort. Real pain. The kind that costs them money, time, relationships, or their sense of who they are. Pain that has made them try to solve the problem before and fail. Pain that comes up in conversation, in forums, in reviews, in the way people vent to friends.

The reason pain intensity matters is urgency. A customer in real pain is actively looking for a solution. A customer in mild discomfort is passively tolerant of the status quo. You want the person who is actively looking, because they are dramatically easier and cheaper to convert. They come to you halfway sold. The customer with mild discomfort needs to be educated, nurtured, and convinced they have a problem worth solving before they'll even consider your solution. That's expensive.

**Question two: Are those people willing and able to spend money?** These are two separate questions that get confused. Willingness without ability means you've found a genuine market of people who can't afford what you'd need to charge. Ability without willingness means the market has convinced itself this problem should be solvable for free. You need both the capacity to spend and the willingness to spend.

The simplest test is to determine if there is already money being spent in this market. Are there existing products, services, subscriptions, and courses being sold? What do they cost? If people are already spending $200 a year in this category, that proves the market. If you can't find evidence of current spending, that's a warning signal.

**Question three: Can you reach the people who have this pain?** The most acute, money-willing market in the world doesn't help you if there's no efficient way to put your message in front of them. Can you find them on forums, in Facebook groups, on YouTube channels, in email lists, at conferences, through podcasts they listen to? The more concentrated and findable the audience, the lower your customer acquisition costs.

## Where to Look for Market Opportunities

The best markets are rarely hidden. They're visible to anyone who knows where to look. The problem is that beginners look in the wrong places. They look at broad industry categories and trend reports rather than at the specific places where real people in specific pain congregate.

Amazon reviews are one of the highest-value, most underused sources of market intelligence available for free. The mechanism is simple. Find a product in the general category you're considering. Read every one-star, two-star, and three-star review. These reviews are a direct window into what the market's existing solutions are failing to deliver. The gap between what the best-rated products in a category promise and what their negative reviews reveal they don't deliver is where your opportunity lives.

When I do this kind of research, I'm not looking for things to criticize about the competitor's product. I'm looking for the pain their product didn't resolve, the thing the customer was hoping would be solved and wasn't. That residual pain is the opportunity.

Reddit is another great source I rely on. The subreddit architecture is essentially an organized directory of human problems. r/personalfinance is a map of financial anxieties. r/relationships is a map of interpersonal struggles. r/DIY is a map of home improvement frustrations. There is a subreddit for almost every niche market, and within those subreddits, real people describe their real problems in their real language, at length, for free.

The specific thing I'm looking for when I read Reddit in a market I'm considering is the recurring thread. The question that gets asked over and over again in slightly different forms. A frustration that comes up in multiple threads from multiple people. These recurring themes in community discussion are the market's unmet needs made visible.

After Amazon and Reddit: Facebook groups (search for groups in your category; they're full of questions and complaints), YouTube comment sections (particularly on how-to videos, where the comments are full of variations of "this didn't work for me because..."), and niche forums specific to the category. Gather this raw material. You're going to bring it to Claude for synthesis.

## Using Claude for Market Discovery

Here is the initial market discovery prompt. I've designed it to produce intelligence you can act on, not vague category descriptions but specific pain points, specific buyer segments, specific reach strategies. Before you run it, spend at least an hour gathering real customer language from the sources I described above. Paste that language into the prompt as context.

**✦ MARKET DISCOVERY PROMPT**

```
I'm evaluating market opportunities in [MARKET CATEGORY – be
specific: not 'health' but 'at-home gut health and
fermentation'].
Below is raw research I've gathered from real customers in
this market (forum posts, Amazon reviews, community
discussions):
[PASTE YOUR GATHERED RESEARCH]
Based on this research AND your broader knowledge of this
market, please analyze:
1. PAIN INTENSITY MAP: List the 8 most significant pain
points in this market, ranked by urgency (how acutely
painful is it?) and spending willingness (are people already
paying to try to solve it?). For each pain point: describe
it in the customer's own language, explain what makes it
acute, and describe what existing solutions fail to deliver.
2. BUYER SEGMENTS: Within this market, identify 3-4
meaningfully different buyer segments. For each: who they
are, what their specific version of the pain is, what
they've already tried, what they'd pay to solve it, and how
you'd reach them.
3. COMPETITIVE LANDSCAPE OVERVIEW: Who are the main existing
solutions in this market? What are their obvious strengths?
What gaps do the pain points you identified reveal in their
offerings?
```

```
4. OPPORTUNITY CANDIDATES: Based on everything above,
describe 3 specific market opportunities (underserved pain
points or underserved segments where a new entrant could
build real traction). For each: the specific customer, the
specific pain, why it's underserved, and what a minimum
viable solution might look like.
5. REACH CHANNELS: For the most promising opportunity you
identified, where does that specific customer congregate
online? List specific forums, subreddits, Facebook groups,
YouTube channels, podcasts, and publications where I would
find them in concentrated, reachable form. Be specific.
Generic market analysis is useless. I want real intelligence
I can act on.
```

**Note:** *The quality of this output is almost entirely determined by the quality of the raw research you paste in. A generic prompt with no research gets generic output. Specific real customer language gets specific, actionable intelligence. Do the gathering work first.*

## Reading the Output: What to Look For

When Claude returns this analysis, you're looking for a few specific signals.

**Pain points with emotional specificity.** "People want to be healthier" is not useful. "People who've followed every gut health protocol on the internet and still have bloating and brain fog feel like their body is working against them, like they've tried everything and nothing works, and the desperation is starting to affect how they show up at work and in their relationships" is useful. The more emotionally specific the pain description, the more real the opportunity.

**Clear evidence of existing spending.** When Claude identifies buyer segments, look for the ones where spending is already demonstrated, where there's evidence of courses, coaches, supplements, or services being sold in the category. Buyer behavior history is far more reliable than stated preferences.

**Gaps that align with your strengths.** The opportunity is most compelling when the underserved pain point is something you specifically know about, can credibly address, or can build expertise in quickly. Not every gap is your gap. Look for the ones where you have a reason to be there.

After reviewing Claude's output, follow up with specific questions on the segments and opportunities that interest you most. Think of the initial analysis as a map and the follow-up questions as the journey.

## A Worked Example

Let me walk you through a simplified version of what this research process produces, so you have a concrete model.

Imagine you're considering the at-home fermentation market. You spend an hour on Amazon reading negative reviews of fermentation kits, an hour on r/fermentation reading recurring questions and complaints, and an hour in Facebook groups watching what people struggle with. You gather the most revealing language from each source and paste it into the market discovery prompt.

Claude's output identifies a pain cluster that keeps appearing: people who are intellectually interested in fermentation, have bought a starter kit or two, but abandoned the practice because they kept having batches fail and couldn't figure out why. The pain isn't just the failed batches. It's the combination of wasted money, wasted effort, and a nagging sense of personal inadequacy. They see confident fermenters posting beautiful jars online and feel like they must be missing something fundamental.

That's a specific, acute, emotional pain with a residual market (people who've already demonstrated buying intent by purchasing their first kit). The reach is excellent, because the communities they're in are visible and accessible. The existing solutions mostly address beginners who want to start fermenting, not people who started and are struggling. That's the gap you're looking for.

From there, you're not building a generic fermentation business, you're building a "fermentation rescue" business for people who've already started and are frustrated. That specific positioning is more compelling, more targetable, and more defensible than a generic "we teach people to ferment" message. And you found it through an hour of research and thirty minutes with Claude.

## Chapter 5: How to Tell if a Market Is Worth Your Time

---

Market size is the question everyone forgets until after they've built something. You find a real pain point.

You validate that people are willing to spend. You build a product and a funnel and a launch plan. You launch. And twelve people buy. The market was real. The pain was real. The product was good. The problem was scale. There weren't enough people with that specific pain to build a sustainable business around it.

Market sizing is the discipline of estimating, before you invest serious time and money, whether the opportunity is large enough to support what you're trying to build. It doesn't need to be precise. Any market size estimate involves assumptions and simplifications. But it needs to be honest, and it needs to confirm that the ceiling on your opportunity is high enough to be worth pursuing.

## Two Approaches, Used Together

There are two approaches to market sizing and they work best in combination.

Top-down sizing starts with the broad market and narrows toward your specific slice. Total US consumer spending on health and wellness is enormous, hundreds of billions annually. The gut health segment within that is a fraction of the total. The home fermentation segment within gut health is a smaller fraction still. Your specific slice, say premium direct-to-consumer kits targeting a specific demographic, is smaller still. But even a small fraction of a large market can be a substantial business.

The top-down approach gives you a sense of whether you're in a large market or a tiny one. A market where you can find meaningful total spending gives you confidence that your fraction, even if small, can support a real business. A market where you struggle to identify any total spending at scale is a warning sign.

Bottom-up sizing starts from the customer unit. Who is your specific customer? How many of them exist? What would a single highly engaged customer realistically spend with you in a year? Multiply those numbers and you get your realistic addressable revenue at meaningful penetration.

The power of the bottom-up approach is that it keeps you honest. It forces you to be specific about who you're selling to and what the realistic economics of that relationship look like. When I do this exercise, I often find that my initial optimism about a market was based on thinking about the total market rather than the specific penetrable slice.

Neither approach produces precise numbers. Together, they produce a range that's useful for decision-making: "this market is at least this large and probably no larger than this, and I need to capture X percent to hit my goals."

**✦ MARKET SIZING PROMPT**

```
I'm sizing the opportunity for a business in [SPECIFIC
MARKET SEGMENT — be specific].
My specific business concept: [DESCRIBE IT — product type,
customer type, channel, price point]
Help me build a sizing estimate using both approaches:
```

```
TOP-DOWN: - What is the size of the total addressable market
(the broad category this fits within)? - What portion does
my specific segment represent? What data or reasoning
supports that estimate? - What growth rate is this segment
on? Is it expanding, stable, or contracting? - What does
this suggest about total spending in my specific slice?
BOTTOM-UP: - Describe my ideal customer in detail. How many
of them exist in [US / specify your market]? - What does a
“light buyer” spend in this category annually? A “moderate
buyer”? A “heavy buyer”? - What is the realistic average
annual spending for a customer in my business specifically?
- What penetration rate (percent of addressable customers)
is realistic for a well-run new entrant in years 1, 2, and
3?
BASED ON BOTH APPROACHES: - Conservative case annual revenue
(Year 1, Year 2, Year 3) - Base case annual revenue (Year 1,
Year 2, Year 3) - Optimistic case annual revenue (Year 1,
Year 2, Year 3)
FINALLY: - Is this a real business or a small lifestyle
business at best? Be honest. - What is the single biggest
factor that would push outcomes toward the optimistic case?
- What is the single biggest factor that would cap outcomes
at the conservative case?
I want honest range estimates, not false precision.
```

**Note:** *Cross-check Claude's output against observable real-world signals. How many reviews do the top Amazon products in this category have? (Volume of reviews correlates with sales volume.) How active are the community forums? How many Google searches happen monthly for the relevant terms? These signals won't give you precise numbers but they'll tell you if Claude's estimates are directionally correct.*

## The Validation Shortcut

All market sizing is hypothesis until someone gives you money.

The fastest and cheapest validation you can do is to build a minimal version of your offer, whether that’s a landing page describing what you’re building, an early-access list, or a pre-sale, and see if real people take an action. Email sign-ups are the minimum bar. Can you get people to give you their email address in exchange for the promise of your product? A purchase before you've built the full product is even better.

Direct response practitioners call this "testing before investing." You're gathering evidence that the market wants what you're planning to build before you invest in building it. Negative evidence at this stage is valuable, because it's teaching you something real at minimum cost. The goal is to fail fast and cheaply on hypotheses that are wrong, so you can invest confidently in the ones that are right.

Build a simple landing page in FunnelKit. Write a two-sentence description of what you're planning to build. Add an opt-in form. Drive traffic to it through a handful of social posts in relevant communities. Give it two weeks. Fifty email sign-ups from targeted traffic is enough to tell you there's a real market. Zero sign-ups from two weeks of consistent effort is enough to tell you something is wrong with the concept, the market, or the targeting.

Those email sign-ups, by the way, are the beginning of your list. The people who said "yes, I want this" are your first audience members and your first prospective customers. Welcome them properly, set expectations about what they'll hear from you next, and remember that a hundred people who asked to hear from you will out-earn a thousand you bought.

## Chapter 6: Flanking — How to Find the Gaps Bigger Competitors Can't Close

Most beginners treat competition as a problem to avoid. They search for markets with no competitors, as if an empty field is a sign of opportunity. It's almost never a good sign. An empty field usually means either that no one wants what's being offered, or that someone already tried and failed for reasons that aren't immediately visible.

Markets with competition are markets where people spend money. The competition proves the demand. Your job isn't to find an empty market, it's to find the angle that lets you win the crowded one.

That angle almost always exists. Even in highly competitive markets, there are underserved customers, pain points, and price points. Finding them is a matter of looking carefully at what the existing players are missing, then asking whether that gap aligns with something you can credibly deliver.

### How to Read the Competition Intelligently

Most people don't do their competitive research properly. They look at what competitors are doing well (their strongest features, their best reviews, their most polished marketing) and conclude either "I can't compete with that" or "I should do what they're doing." Neither conclusion is useful.

The right approach is to look for what competitors are consistently failing at. What complaints recur in their reviews? What questions appear in community forums that their products don't answer? What customer segments are they clearly not designed for? What price point are they ignoring? These are your openings.

The principle behind this approach is simple: large, successful companies are optimized around their core customer, which means they're systematically under-optimized for everyone else. A market leader who built their business serving professional fermenters is probably not serving the frustrated beginner particularly well. They don't have to, because they're making great money from their primary segment. But that leaves a real gap.

Your job is to find the gap and own it with more conviction than the market leader could muster even if they tried.

**✦ COMPETITIVE ANALYSIS PROMPT**

```
I'm analyzing the competitive landscape in [YOUR MARKET].
I've gathered the following research on the main players:
[PASTE COMPETITOR INFORMATION — product descriptions,
pricing, reviews especially negative ones, community
mentions, perceived strengths and weaknesses. The more
specific the better.]
Based on this research plus your knowledge of this market,
please provide:
1. COMPETITIVE MAP: Describe how the main players are
positioned. For each significant player: who they primarily
serve, what their core value proposition is, where they are
strong, and where they are consistently criticized or weak.
2. TABLE STAKES: What do all the main players get right?
What would I need to match just to be considered a viable
option? (These are the baseline requirements. Being better
than them here won't win, but being worse will disqualify
you.)
```

```
3. SYSTEMATIC GAPS: What pain points or customer segments
keep appearing in the research that NO current player
adequately serves? These are the market's unfulfilled needs
and the most valuable intelligence in this analysis.
4. POSITIONING WINDOWS: Based on the gaps, describe 3
specific positioning territories a new entrant could occupy.
For each: who exactly it serves, what the core promise would
be, why existing players aren't there (what structural
reason prevents them from simply copying it), and how
defensible it is over time.
5. COMPETITIVE RISK ASSESSMENT: If I entered this market and
started gaining traction, what would the most dangerous
competitive response look like? How do I build in defenses
against that response?
6. THE RECOMMENDED ENTRY POINT: Of everything you've
analyzed, where is the most attractive opening for a smart
new entrant with limited budget? Make a recommendation and
explain the reasoning.
Don't be polite about gaps or weaknesses. I need honest
competitive intelligence.
```

**Note:** *This analysis is most valuable when you've done genuine research first. Read actual reviews, participate in actual communities, buy and use competitor products if possible. The more specific your inputs, the more specific and actionable the outputs.*

### The Flanking Strategy

There's a classical military concept called flanking. Instead of attacking the enemy's strongest position head-on, you move around to their flank, the position they haven't defended because they're focused on the front.

In business, flanking means going after the customer segment the dominant players have ignored because it doesn't fit their core business model. The segment that's too small for the market leader to care about, but large enough to build a real business in.

Southwest Airlines didn't try to out-luxury American or Delta. They flanked them entirely by owning the low-cost, high-reliability positioning that the legacy carriers had structurally abandoned in their pursuit of premium revenue. FedEx didn't try to beat UPS on volume. They owned the "absolutely, positively overnight" positioning that UPS wasn't specifically committed to. In both cases, the winning move was to find the position the market leader would have to dismantle their existing business to contest.

When you look at your competitive landscape with Claude's help, look specifically for that kind of opening: the customer segment the market leaders are under-serving not because they tried and failed, but because it doesn't fit their business model. Once you've found it, the question becomes whether you can serve it credibly and whether it's big enough to build on. Those are answerable questions, and the answers will tell you whether you've found your market.

# Chapter 7: The Customer Avatar — Knowing One Person Well Enough to Sell to Thousands

---

Every piece of copy you write, every email you send, every offer you design, every funnel you build is a message to a specific person. Not a demographic segment. Not a user persona in a deck. A specific human being, sitting somewhere, with specific feelings about their specific problem, reading what you wrote on a specific device in a specific context.

The customer avatar is your attempt to know that person well enough that when they read your copy, they feel like you know them. Like you somehow understood their situation without being told. That feeling of being understood is the most powerful thing in marketing. It converts better than any headline formula or urgency tactic.

And it's hard to manufacture. You can't research your way into it from demographic reports. You can't generalize your way to it from market categories. It comes from genuine, specific curiosity about a specific human being: their fears, their failures, their identity, their language, their hopes for what's on the other side of the problem.

Claude can help you build the avatar systematically. But the raw material, the real customer language you've gathered from forums and reviews and conversations, is the thing that makes the avatar come to life rather than remaining theoretical.

## Demographics Vs. Psychographics

Demographic data (age, gender, income, location, education) tells you something useful. It helps you understand financial constraints, cultural context, and where to find people. But demographics explain almost nothing about buying behavior.

Two people who are demographically identical, with the same age, income, and education level, can have completely opposite responses to the same marketing message. Because buying decisions are driven by psychology: values, identity, fear, aspiration, past experience, and self-image.

Psychographic data gets at these drivers. What do they believe about themselves? What community do they belong to and what does that membership mean to them? What have they tried before and what story do they tell themselves about why it didn't work? What would success look like to them, specifically, and how would it change how they feel about themselves?

These are the questions that produce copy that lands. Demographics get you in the room. Psychographics are what make the person in the room feel like you're talking directly to them.

**✦ CUSTOMER AVATAR PROMPT**

```
I'm building a detailed customer avatar for my business in
[YOUR MARKET].
My specific product/service is [DESCRIBE IT].
Here is real language I've gathered from potential customers
in this market (forum posts, reviews, social media),
verbatim: [PASTE YOUR GATHERED CUSTOMER LANGUAGE – the more
raw and real, the better]
Using this language as your primary source, build a detailed
customer avatar:
DEMOGRAPHICS (brief – this is just context, not the
important part): - Age range, gender, income, life stage
PSYCHOGRAPHICS (this is where the important insights live):
- What does this person value most? What principles guide
their decisions about spending, time, and attention? - How
do they see themselves? What is their self-concept? What do
they want to be seen as by others? - What communities do
they belong to and what does belonging to those communities
mean to them? - What are they proud of? What are they
ashamed of? Both matter for marketing.
```

```
THE PAIN: - Describe the central problem in full detail. Not
just what it is, but what it feels like, how long they've
had it, how it affects their daily life, what they've tried,
why those attempts failed. - What does the problem cost
them, financially, emotionally, in their relationships, in
their self-image? - What moment typically triggers them to
actively look for a solution?
THE DESIRE: - If this problem were fully solved, what would
their life look like? Paint a specific emotional picture,
not just functional outcomes. - What would they say about
themselves if they'd solved it? How would they describe the
change to a friend?
BUYING PSYCHOLOGY: - What objections stand between them and
purchasing? What are they afraid of? - Who and what do they
trust? Where do they get recommendations? - What marketing
approaches make them roll their eyes or feel manipulated?
LANGUAGE: - What exact phrases, from the research I
provided, do they use to describe their problem? List them
verbatim. - What words do they use that they NEVER hear in
marketing for this category?
FINAL EXERCISE: Write a 300-word "day in the life" narrative
from this person's perspective. First person, on a day when
the problem is particularly acute. Show the emotional
texture of the problem, not just the functional description.
```

**Note:** *The "day in the life" section is the most useful part of this output. Read it carefully. Look for the specific moment when your product would appear, when it would intersect their life and change something. That moment is the emotional core of your best copy.*

## Just One Avatar

New business owners want to build many avatars because they're afraid of excluding potential customers. Every time I work with someone on this and suggest they commit to a single avatar, they push back: "But we could also serve X type of person, and Y type of person, and..."

Writing to one specific person is how you reach many people effectively. When you speak to one person with deep specificity and genuine understanding, everyone who resembles that person feels spoken to. The copy that resonates with your avatar resonates with everyone like your avatar.

Trying to write to ten different people simultaneously means you speak to none of them effectively. The copy becomes generic, smooth, inoffensive, forgettable. Nobody reads it and thinks "that was written for me."

Commit to one avatar. The most important one: the person who, if you got them as a customer, would be the most valuable, most likely to buy again, most likely to refer others. Build everything for that person first. Once you have traction and revenue and real data coming in, you'll have earned the right to expand to a second avatar, then a third.

## Interlude: What This Looks Like in Practice — Five Case Studies

---

*The case studies in this chapter include one genuine consulting engagement and four composite examples based on typical results across real business types. The composites are labeled clearly.*

### The Consulting Case: When Every Standard Channel Is Closed

The four composite examples below cover the playbook when standard paid channels are available. This consulting case covers the situation when they are not, when the category itself makes every conventional advertising platform unavailable, and the system has to find a different answer.

## CONSULTING CASE: Specialty Hemp Genetics Brand

*Direct-to-Consumer — Solving a Total Channel Lockout with List Building and a Viral Ambassador Program*

#### THE CHANNEL PROBLEM

In forty years of direct response work, I have run into hard problems: categories with thin margins, offers with terrible conversion economics, clients who had built their business on a single channel that suddenly stopped working. This one was in a different category. The client ran a specialty hemp genetics business with a devoted collector community, genuine word-of-mouth appeal, and a product people actively recommended to friends. He had almost no viable paid advertising channels, because the category is systematically blocked across virtually every major platform. Facebook and Instagram rejected ads in the category regardless of how the creative was framed. Google Ads, rejected. Yahoo, rejected. Most programmatic display networks, restricted or banned. Instagram was throttling his organic content on top of refusing paid placement, so posts that should have reached his followers were being suppressed at the algorithm level. He had tried every conventional channel a direct-to-consumer brand would reach for, and every door was closed. When he came to me, he had a passionate customer base, a strong product, and no scalable way to reach new buyers. It was a genuinely difficult problem.

#### HOW CLAUDE BUILT THE PROGRAM

The channel lockout pointed to a strategic pivot that felt almost counterintuitive in an era of paid traffic: go old school. Build the list. Make the existing customers do the selling. If the platforms won't let you reach strangers, build a system that turns your best customers into a voluntary sales force, and give them enough reason to recruit actively. The client had approximately 800 members in a dedicated online community, people who had been buying for years and who regularly mentioned the brand in broader enthusiast forums. They were already talking. The job was to give them a structure that made their advocacy trackable, rewarded, and scalable. An ambassador program. Building that program from scratch, including the recruitment strategy, the copy for every touchpoint, the milestone ladder, the tracking infrastructure, and the automated sequences that fire at each milestone, would have been a months-long agency project at serious cost. With Claude, the entire system was designed, written, and ready to deploy in three weeks of focused work. The first Claude session mapped the program architecture: a tiered milestone system at 1, 5, 10, 25, and 50 referrals, with rewards escalating at each level and a Platinum tier at 50 referrals that unlocked a quarterly curated package delivered directly to the ambassador. The recruitment email sequence, four emails over two weeks, was drafted by Claude from detailed prompts about the community's language, the specific objections likely to surface, and the emotional tone of a collector community that is skeptical of anything that feels like a corporate program. These are people who know each other. They can tell when they're being sold to. Every email was edited heavily for authenticity, but the structural logic of the sequence (the right sequence of messages, the right angle for each one, the right moment to introduce each element of the program) came from the Claude sessions. Claude also wrote every automated email in the system: the enrollment welcome, the milestone notifications at each tier, the near-miss nudges when an ambassador was one referral away from leveling up, and the full Platinum welcome sequence. FunnelKit handled the infrastructure: the ambassador enrollment landing page, the opt-in and registration flow, and all automated sequences. The entire platform cost under $30 a month to run.

**THE RESULTS**

The initial recruitment email went to the 805-person community list. The response was so strong the client had to shut the program down to handle the volume. Sixty-two ambassadors enrolled. That's a 7.7% response rate from a list of existing customers who had never been asked to participate in anything like this before — and these were the results out of the gate, with no testing, no refinement, no optimization. The acquisition numbers were where it got interesting. The ambassador network drove 527 new email addresses into the business in the first few days. Each one was acquired through a trusted personal recommendation rather than a cold ad. Each one entered a 120-day drip campaign for ongoing nurture. The bump revenue from the lead generation totaled $1,482 and the upsell revenue added another $629 — and those numbers came on top of a break-even free plus shipping offer and before any of the lifetime value from those 527 new subscribers had a chance to materialize. The referral economics were favorable in a way paid channels can't match. Leads were acquired at a PROFIT of over $5 each when the goal was to try to get as close to break-even as possible. The customers who arrived through referral had materially higher retention because they came pre-sold by someone they trusted. The program became the client's primary new customer acquisition channel — the only one that worked at scale given the platform restrictions on the underlying business. And the numbers above are first-week, untuned, no-iteration results with lots of room to improve.

**KEY LESSON**

When every conventional paid channel is closed, the most powerful acquisition asset you have is the trust your existing customers already have with people like them. The ambassador program worked not because it was clever but because it activated something that was already there: genuine enthusiasm, community belonging, and the human instinct to share things worth knowing about. Claude made building the infrastructure to harness that activation faster and cheaper than any alternative. The list-building and ambassador approach is slower than paid traffic at the start. Over twelve months, it compounds in ways that paid traffic never does, because every ambassador the program produces recruits more ambassadors, and the trust embedded in a peer referral cannot be bought at any CPC rate.

## Four Composite Examples Across Business Types

### COMPOSITE CASE STUDY: Meridian Home Remodeling

*Local Service — Appointment-Setting Funnel*

**THE SITUATION**

A regional home remodeling contractor generating leads primarily through word of mouth and occasional yard signs. The owner was booking two to three consultation appointments per week, closing roughly forty percent of them at an average project value of $18,000. The business was profitable but fully dependent on the owner's personal network for growth.

**HOW THEY USED CLAUDE**

Using Claude, the owner developed a lead magnet specifically targeting the concern most common in his market: homeowners who suspected their bathroom or kitchen was overdue for renovation but weren't sure whether the scope justified the cost. The lead magnet was a two-page PDF guide called "The Five Signs Your Kitchen Is Costing You More Than a Renovation Would," written in a single two-hour Claude session that started with a detailed prompt about his avatar, their specific fears, and the language they used in consultations. Claude produced a draft; the owner edited it to add three specific anecdotes from real projects he had completed. The final guide was specific, credible, and directly connected to the service he was selling.

#### THE RESULTS

Within ninety days, the funnel was generating eight to twelve consultation requests per week from paid traffic at approximately $22 per lead. His close rate held at thirty-eight percent. Average project value increased to $21,500 as the funnel attracted homeowners who were more actively researching the decision and therefore further along in their decision process. Monthly revenue increased roughly sixty percent over the prior six-month average.

#### KEY LESSON

The lead magnet worked because it addressed a specific decision the customer was already making, not because it was long or technically sophisticated. Two pages, written in two hours, and the economics of his entire lead generation system reshaped themselves around that small asset over the following quarter.

### COMPOSITE CASE STUDY: Coastal Provisions

*Physical Product — Product Selling Funnel with Order Bump and Upsell*

#### THE SITUATION

A small-batch artisan hot sauce brand selling at farmers markets and through a basic e-commerce site. Monthly revenue was approximately $3,200, almost entirely from returning customers and market regulars. Average order value was $18. The founder had a product people loved but no system for consistently converting new customers.

#### HOW THEY USED CLAUDE

The first Claude session focused on the avatar: who specifically was the ideal first-time buyer, what did they already believe about hot sauce, what frustrated them about commercial brands, what did they say when they recommended a favorite product to a friend. From that session came the copy direction for every page in the funnel. Not generic "premium artisan" language, but specific claims grounded in the things customers actually said. The free-plus-shipping offer was redesigned around a single sampler bottle at no cost with shipping covered, positioned as "the way people actually discover us: by trying it, not by reading about it."

#### THE RESULTS

Average order value increased from $18 to $34 within sixty

days of the funnel launching, driven primarily by an upsell take rate of twenty-two percent and an order bump take rate of thirty-one percent. Monthly revenue climbed to approximately $7,800 over the following six months as the owner incrementally increased ad spend with confidence in the funnel economics. Email open rates on the welcome sequence averaged forty-one percent, well above the e-commerce industry average.

**KEY LESSON**

The digital order bump was a PDF guide that cost nothing to produce and nothing to fulfill, and it became the highest-margin product in the lineup. Without Claude this would have been a time-consuming deliverable, but well-prompted this gets knocked out in an afternoon. The broader lesson is that the economics of order bumps change completely when the incremental product is digital: your margin approaches 100 percent, fulfillment cost drops to zero, and suddenly an extra $9 on every checkout is almost pure profit.

## COMPOSITE CASE STUDY: The Bookkeeping Bureau

*B2B Service — Lead Generation and Nurture Funnel*

**THE SITUATION**

A solo bookkeeping practitioner serving small business clients, generating two to three new clients per month through accountant referrals. Average monthly retainer was $420. The practitioner had capacity for ten to twelve additional clients but no systematic way to fill those slots without referral partners who had their own business to run.

**HOW THEY USED CLAUDE**

The avatar work identified a specific target: small business owners in their second or third year who were profitable but increasingly anxious about their tax exposure and financial visibility. Their primary fear wasn't that they were failing. It was that they didn't know whether they were failing or succeeding. Claude helped develop a lead magnet targeting that exact anxiety: "Seven Numbers Every Profitable Small Business Owner Should Know (and Most Don't)." The guide was technically specific, covering gross margin percentage, owner's compensation ratio, accounts receivable days, and four others, with a one-paragraph explanation of what each number revealed and what the dangerous range looked like. It was genuinely useful content that demonstrated expertise without selling anything.

**THE RESULTS**

Within four months, the funnel was generating fifteen to twenty qualified opt-ins per week from LinkedIn content driving traffic to the lead magnet page. Approximately twelve percent of subscribers booked an introductory call, and the practitioner closed sixty percent of those calls. Monthly new client acquisition increased from two to three clients to five to seven. The average retainer also increased as the funnel attracted clients who were more financially sophisticated and therefore more willing to invest in ongoing support.

**KEY LESSON**

The email sequence that converted best was email four, a specific, honest description of the three financial mistakes the practitioner saw most often in new client files. Written with Claude and heavily edited for her specific voice and observations, it generated the most replies of any email in the sequence and was the most commonly cited reason new clients gave for booking a call. What would a new client say made them pick up the phone — usually email four.

## COMPOSITE CASE STUDY: Aperture Academy

*Digital Product — Course Funnel with Lead Magnet and Email Sequence*

**THE SITUATION**

A professional photographer with twelve thousand Instagram followers and a reputation in the enthusiast photography community had been considering a course on composition and visual storytelling for two years. He had the knowledge. He lacked the marketing infrastructure and the confidence that an audience would pay for what he knew.

**HOW THEY USED CLAUDE**

The first Claude session was devoted entirely to the customer avatar, specifically the photographer who was two to three years into a serious hobby, producing technically competent images, and frustrated that the images weren't connecting emotionally with viewers. That frustration became the center of everything: the lead magnet title, the email sequence, the course positioning. The lead magnet, a free email mini-course called "Five Compositions That Create Instant Emotional Impact," delivered one specific, implementable composition technique per day over five days, with before-and-after examples and a specific practice exercise for each. Claude wrote the first draft of each lesson from detailed notes; the photographer edited each one to add specific images from his portfolio and specific observations from his own learning.

#### THE RESULTS

Within ninety days of launching the funnel with modest paid traffic ($400 total in Facebook ads), the list had grown to 2,400 subscribers with an average opt-in cost of $0.17. The course launch to that list generated sixty-one sales at $297, totaling $18,117. A second launch to a larger list six weeks later generated ninety-three sales. The paid ads that seeded the initial list cost less than 1.5% of the revenue from a single sale.

#### KEY LESSON

The five-day mini-course worked because it delivered something genuinely valuable before asking for anything. By day five, subscribers had implemented real techniques and seen real improvement in their own images. The $297 course was an easy next step for people who had already gotten results from the free content, which is exactly the architecture the welcome sequence is designed to create.

# Part Three: Think Like a Strategist

# Chapter 8: The Three Growth Levers (And Why Most Businesses Only Use One)

---

The three-lever framework comes from the core of direct response discipline, forty years of measuring campaigns, tracking results, and identifying the patterns that separate businesses that grow from businesses that grind.

I came to it embarrassingly late. When I finally worked through the framework carefully, I went back through my business history and could see exactly where I'd been doing things right without understanding why, exactly where I'd been leaving money on the table, and exactly where my strategic errors were. The clarity was valuable, but the real value was prospective: using the framework to plan better before building, rather than analyzing after the fact.

There are three ways to grow any business. Every growth strategy you'll ever encounter is a variation on one of them. Understanding these three levers changes how you think about every marketing decision you make.

## The Three Levers

**Lever One: Get more customers.** More people transact with you for the first time. Advertising, content marketing, SEO, partnerships, referrals; all of these are lever one activities. You're expanding the top of the funnel.

**Lever Two: Increase the value of each transaction.** When someone buys from you, they spend more. Order bumps, upsells, cross-sells, premium versions, bundling; all lever two. You're making each sale more valuable without necessarily getting more sales.

**Lever Three: Increase how often customers buy.** Email marketing, loyalty programs, subscriptions, community building, win-back campaigns — all lever three. You're getting each customer to come back more times over their lifetime with you.

That's it. Those are the only three ways to grow revenue. Every tactic you've ever heard of is a specific variation on one or more of these three levers.

## Why These Levers Are Not Equal

The profound strategic insight in the three-lever framework is the economics. They are dramatically different in cost and efficiency, but most businesses are focusing almost all their energy on the most expensive one.

Lever one, getting new customers, is expensive. You're paying to reach strangers, convince them to trust you enough to try you, and convert them through an entire purchase process. Customer acquisition costs vary widely by industry and channel, but in almost every market, acquiring a new customer costs significantly more than selling again to an existing one. This is the lever that consumes the majority of most businesses' marketing budgets.

Lever two, higher transaction value, is dramatically cheaper. The customer is already in the buying moment. They've already decided to purchase. Getting them to add something, upgrade something, or buy more in the same transaction requires a fraction of the persuasion cost of the original sale. A well-executed order bump on the checkout page costs you nothing to present and typically increases average order value by fifteen to thirty percent.

Lever three, more frequent purchase, is also underinvested by most businesses. An existing customer who has already bought from you and had a good experience is dramatically more likely to buy again than a cold prospect. The communication cost of staying in front of existing customers (email marketing, primarily) is tiny compared to the cost of acquiring new ones.

Here's the math: a twenty percent improvement in each of the three levers compounds to a seventy-three percent revenue increase. Not seventy-three percent total, but a seventy-three percent increase over baseline. Three modest improvements, applied simultaneously, nearly double revenue. Run the arithmetic yourself if you don't believe it: $1.2 \times 1.2 \times 1.2 = 1.728$.

### The Strategic Implication

If you're focused primarily on getting more traffic, more leads, and more first-time customers, while neglecting the transaction value and frequency levers, you're on a treadmill. You need to keep acquiring customers at full cost just to maintain revenue, let alone grow it.

The business that activates all three levers simultaneously grows geometrically with the same traffic volume, and the one with superior economics on levers two and three can afford to spend more to acquire each customer on lever one, which means it can outcompete on advertising, on partnerships, on visibility, because its downstream revenue supports that investment.

This is why building the upsell sequence before you scale traffic isn't backwards. It's how sophisticated businesses approach growth. Get the economics right at the customer level, then scale the customer acquisition. Everything works in that direction and nothing works as well in the other.

**✦ THREE LEVERS STRATEGY PROMPT**

```
I'm planning the growth strategy for my business. Here's the
full context:
BUSINESS: [What you sell, who you sell to, what it costs]
CURRENT STATE: [Where you are now – any existing customers,
any existing list, any existing revenue]
GOALS: [What you want to achieve in the next 12 months]
CONSTRAINTS: [Budget, time, skills, anything else that
limits what's available to you]
Please analyze my business using the three-lever framework
and give me a specific growth plan:
```

```
LEVER ONE – MORE CUSTOMERS: - What are the 3 most efficient
customer acquisition channels for this specific business at
this stage? - What lead generation approach makes the most
sense? What should I offer to get people into my world
before asking them to buy? - What does a realistic cost-per-
acquisition look like, and what first-purchase revenue do I
need to break even on acquisition? - What is the realistic
timeline to meaningful volume on each channel?
LEVER TWO – HIGHER TRANSACTION VALUE: - What are the most
natural upsell and cross-sell opportunities for this
product? - What order bump makes sense on the checkout page?
- What one-click upsell should fire immediately after
purchase? - What is the pricing architecture: entry offer,
core offer, premium tier? - If I execute lever two well,
what does average order value look like vs. a single-product
sale?
LEVER THREE – MORE FREQUENT PURCHASE: - What email marketing
approach keeps this customer engaged and drives repeat
purchase? - How often would a highly engaged customer
realistically buy, and what would drive that frequency? - Is
there a subscription or membership model that makes sense
here? What would it offer? - What's the realistic repeat
purchase rate for this product category, and how do I
maximize it?
SEQUENCING: Given where I am right now, which lever should I
prioritize first, and in what order should I build out the
others? Give me a specific 90-day sequence.
```

**Note:** *Pay close attention to the sequencing recommendation. Most new businesses should build lever two (transaction value) before scaling lever one (customer acquisition). There's no point pouring water into a leaky bucket. Get the per-customer economics right, then increase the volume.*

◆ *The three-lever framework is the strategic foundation of the One-Person Marketing Department. Every growth decision you make from here forward can be examined through it: which lever does this move? At what cost? What is the downstream effect on the other two? Most strategic mistakes, when you look at them afterwards, turn out to be a move on one lever that quietly hurt another. The framework is a way of seeing those tradeoffs before you commit to them.*

# Chapter 9: Positioning — How to Stop Competing on Price

Positioning is the one strategic decision that affects everything else downstream. Your positioning determines who you're selling to, what you say to them, what you charge, who you hire, what you build, and whether you grow or grind.

Most businesses default to generic positioning without realizing it. They describe themselves in terms that could apply to any competitor: "high quality," "great service," "results-focused," "customer-centric." These claims communicate nothing because every business makes them. Customers hear them and their brain translates them directly to: "this is a generic business I have no particular reason to choose over any other."

Strong positioning is specific, differentiated, and addressed to a specific person — it answers three questions with precision: who exactly you serve, what exactly you do for them, and why you're the right choice for this specific thing rather than the alternatives.

## The Strategy of Preeminence

The Strategy of Preeminence is something I learned decades ago from legendary marketing genius Jay Abraham, and it goes beyond positioning as most people understand it. It's not just about how you're different from competitors, it's about the fundamental relationship you want to have with your customer.

Most businesses conceive of themselves as vendors: providers of products or services in exchange for money. The transaction is the entire relationship. This approach argues for a different self-concept — the trusted advisor.

The trusted advisor isn't in a transactional relationship. They're in a relationship of genuine investment in the customer's outcomes. They tell customers what they need, even when it's not the most expensive option. They proactively share relevant information rather than waiting to be asked. They're invested in the customer's success rather than just the sale.

This shift in self-concept, from vendor to trusted advisor, changes everything about how you communicate, how you design your offers, how you handle objections, and how you treat existing customers, and it produces dramatically better business results because people can feel the difference. They will buy from trusted advisors with far less resistance than they buy from vendors.

When you build your Unique Selling Proposition (USP) and your positioning, do it through the lens of the Strategy of Preeminence. Ask not "what makes us different from competitors?" but "what would make someone with this problem feel that we are the obvious, trusted resource for their situation?" That question produces better positioning every time.

**✦ USP AND POSITIONING PROMPT**

```
I'm developing my business positioning and Unique Selling
Proposition. Here's my full context:
MARKET AND SEGMENT: [Your specific market and the sub-
segment you're targeting]
CUSTOMER AVATAR: [One paragraph – their core pain, what
they've tried, what success looks like, their identity]
COMPETITIVE CONTEXT: [What existing solutions do, what they
miss, why your customer is still looking]
MY GENUINE CAPABILITIES: [What you know, have, or can do
that is specifically different – be honest about what's real
here, not aspirational]
Please help me develop strong positioning by:
1. POSITIONING TERRITORY: Based on competitive gaps and my
customer's unfulfilled desires, what positioning territory
is available and defensible for me? Where specifically is
the open space?
2. USP CANDIDATES: Generate 6 candidate USP statements. Each
must: - Be specific enough that it cannot apply to any other
business - Make a promise the customer deeply wants - Be
something I can deliver credibly - Create exclusivity; it
should implicitly exclude customers who aren't the right fit
Rate each on specificity, credibility, and desirability.
3. THE ONLY WE STATEMENT: Complete this exactly: "We are the
only [type of business] that [specific differentiator] for
[specific customer description]." This should be something
literally true. If you can't make it literally true, the
positioning needs more work.
4. STRATEGY OF PREEMINENCE STATEMENT: Write a 3-sentence
internal positioning statement that captures: who we are at
our best, who we serve, and the relationship we're committed
to having with our customer. This is the internal compass,
not a tagline.
5. POSITIONING STRESS TEST: Play devil's advocate. What are
the weaknesses in this positioning? What would a skeptical
potential customer question? What would a smart competitor
do to undermine it?
6. THE BEST ONE: From everything above, which positioning
direction is strongest for long-term business building? Make
a clear recommendation with reasoning.
```

**Note:** *The "Only We" test is the most valuable part. If you can complete that sentence with something true and specific, you have real positioning. If the sentence rings hollow, or if you can't fill in all three parts with real, specific content, you need more differentiation before you build your marketing.*

## Owned Territory

The goal of positioning is to own a territory: a specific place in your customer's mind that you occupy so completely that alternatives feel like settling.

You own territory by making a specific promise and keeping it everywhere. Your landing pages, your emails, your customer service, your product, your refund policy — every touchpoint either reinforces your positioning or contradicts it. There's no neutral ground.

The businesses I admire most maintain consistency with their positioning. You can read any piece of their communication and know immediately who it's from, because the positioning is so embedded in the execution that it's unmistakable.

That level of consistency isn't achieved by writing a positioning statement and then forgetting about it. It's achieved by using the positioning as a filter for every decision. Does this email reinforce our positioning? Does this offer design support or undermine it? Does the way we handle this customer service situation affirm the relationship we've promised? Those are questions you'll end up asking a hundred times a year, and the answers compound across every touchpoint into the kind of brand that feels unmistakably like itself.

# Chapter 10: The Hero Framework — How to Build Real Authority in Your Market

---

### A Note on Influence

If you've read Russell Brunson's *Expert Secrets,* you'll recognize some of the DNA in what follows. His concept of the Attractive Character, the idea that a consistent, authentic human personality at the center of a business outperforms faceless brand marketing, was one of the clearest early articulations of what I'm calling the Hero framework. His thinking influenced mine, and I'd rather say so than not.

What I'm presenting here extends that foundation and frames it specifically for the AI-augmented workflow, for the operator using Claude to produce the content and copy that expresses the Hero's voice at scale. If the Hero chapter resonates with you, *Expert Secrets* is worth your time alongside it.

People don't follow brands, they follow people.

This is the most important thing to understand about email marketing, about content marketing, about community building, about selling anything online to anyone who has choices. The businesses that build rabid, loyal, buying audiences are almost always built around a specific human voice: a character with a point of view, a history, a way of seeing things, and a consistent way of showing up.

That character is what I call the Hero of the business. This isn't a mascot or a persona in the marketing-jargon sense. I'm talking about a genuine, consistent human identity that your audience comes to know, trust, and look forward to hearing from.

In some businesses, the Hero is the founder themselves, a real person whose genuine story and voice is the central brand asset. In others, the Hero is a carefully constructed character who embodies the brand values in a specific, consistent way. In either case, the effect on the business is the same: a recognizable, trustworthy voice makes everything downstream (the copy, the emails, the offers, the community) work dramatically better than it would from a faceless brand.

This chapter is about building your Hero, and about the drip campaign, which is the Hero's primary tool for building the relationship that makes selling feel easy.

## The Six Elements of a Hero Identity

A Hero identity has six elements. Each one, defined clearly and used consistently, builds the cumulative impression that makes your audience feel like they know you personally, even if they have never met you, even if they are one of fifty thousand people on your list.

**Origin story.** Why did you start this? What happened to you that led you here? Every effective brand Hero has an origin story that is specific, honest, and resonant. Not the polished LinkedIn version but the real version, with the messy middle where things went wrong, where you tried something and it failed, where you got the information or experience that changed your direction. The origin story is the foundation of trust because it shows vulnerability and specificity, which are the two things brands almost never do.

**Core beliefs.** What are your core beliefs that people in your market don't necessarily embrace or agree with? Every effective Hero has a strong point of view about how things should be done, about what the market gets wrong, about what matters most. These beliefs are not brand positioning statements written by a committee, they are convictions held by a person. When you articulate your beliefs clearly, people who share them feel immediately and deeply understood, and those that don't self-select out, which is also healthy.

**Voice and tone.** How do you talk? What is the rhythm of your sentences? Do you use humor? How dark or light is that humor? Are you earnest or sardonic? Do you swear? Do you use technical language or street language? The voice should be yours, not performed, not aspirational. When people read your emails, they should hear you, not some generic corporate speak without a soul.

**Your expertise.** What do you know that other people in your space don't? Not the broad category. The specific corner where your knowledge is hard-won and theirs is borrowed from somewhere else. The Hero isn't a generalist. The Hero stakes out a corner and owns it.

**Who you serve.** The Hero exists for a specific person, not a one-size-fits-all for a demographic. A type of person with a specific kind of struggle — the Hero knows who that person is, what keeps them up at night, and what success looks like for them. This clarity about who you serve shapes everything the Hero says.

**Mission.** What are you ultimately trying to build or change? The business isn't the mission, it's just the mechanism. The mission has to be bigger than revenue to resonate with your audience. A fitness coach's mission might be to prove that people over fifty don't have to accept physical decline as inevitable. A freelance business course creator's mission might be to make the knowledge that agencies charge enormous fees for available to any individual with a laptop and work ethic. The mission gives the Hero a reason to exist beyond making money, and audiences can feel the difference.

**✦ HERO IDENTITY DEVELOPMENT PROMPT**

```
I need to develop the Hero identity for my business, the
consistent brand persona that will be the voice of all my
communications.
Here is my raw material:
BUSINESS: [What you sell, who you sell to, the category you
are in]
MY REAL STORY: [The actual origin – what happened to you,
what you tried, what failed, what worked, what brought you
here]
MY GENUINE BELIEFS: [Things you believe about your market
that most people do not fully say out loud]
MY VOICE AS I EXPERIENCE IT: [How I talk – formal or casual,
serious or funny, cursing or not, long sentences or short,
etc.]
MY CUSTOMER: [Who they are, what they struggle with, what
they want]
Build my complete Hero identity:
1. ORIGIN STORY (two versions): - Full version (400 words):
the complete story as it would appear in an about page or
first email - Short version (80 words): the compressed
version for use in bios, subject lines, and references
What to include: the moment of failure or frustration that
started the journey, the specific discovery or change, the
result that followed, why this matters for the reader.
2. CORE BELIEFS (manifesto format): Write five specific
```

```
things my Hero believes about the industry, the customer, or
the way things should be done. Each belief should be
specific enough to make some people uncomfortable. It should
represent a genuine position, not a platitude.
Format: "I believe that..." statements. Each with one
sentence of explanation.
3. VOICE DESCRIPTION: Write a one-paragraph description of
the Hero voice that could be used to brief any writer or AI
tool. Include: sentence length and rhythm, use of humor,
level of formality, specific things the Hero says and never
says, emotional register, relationship with the reader.
4. THE HERO STATEMENT: Complete this: "I am [who you are]
who [what you do] for [who you serve] because [why it
matters beyond the business]." This is the internal compass
statement, not a tagline, not a pitch, but the true north of
the brand.
5. VOICE SAMPLE: Write a 200-word email opening in the
Hero's voice on a completely mundane topic: a Tuesday
morning, a coffee, an observation about something ordinary.
This is a pure voice exercise. There should be no selling in
it. It should sound unmistakably like the Hero.
```

**Note:** *The voice sample is the most important output from this prompt. Read it out loud. Does it sound like you? Does it sound like someone you would want to read an email from? If the answer to either question is no, give Claude specific feedback on what is wrong. The voice is the product, in a real sense. Get it right before you start writing emails.*

## Why the Hero Changes Everything About Your Email

Here is the problem with most business email: it sounds like it came from a company, not a person. It uses passive constructions and corporate politeness. It leads with "I hope this finds you well." It talks about the product in the third person. It hedges everything. It is inoffensive and completely unmemorable.

Nobody looks forward to receiving this email. They don't search their inbox for it when they haven't heard from you in a while. Nobody tells their friends about it. It just sits there, getting opened occasionally, clicked sometimes, generating mediocre results that feel like the ceiling when they are just the floor.

The Hero changes this by making the email feel like it comes from a person the reader has a genuine relationship with. When people know the Hero's story, when they have read the core beliefs and found themselves nodding, when the voice is distinctive enough that they recognize it from the first sentence, then the email is not a marketing message. It is a letter from someone they want to hear from. This is all about creating a connection with your audience.

This shift in how the email is received changes every metric downstream. Open rates go up because people recognize the sender name and look forward to what they say. Click rates go up because readers trust the Hero's recommendations. Conversion rates go up because the offer doesn't come from a stranger, it comes from someone who has demonstrated expertise and genuine investment in the reader's success over many emails.

The mechanics of implementing this are simpler than they sound. You write the Hero identity first. Then you run every email through the question: does this sound like the Hero? If yes, publish, if no, fix it. That's the whole discipline.

## The Drip Campaign: Where the Hero Lives

The drip campaign is the long-running automated email sequence that every subscriber enters after completing the welcome sequence. It runs indefinitely, delivering value consistently, building the Hero's relationship with the reader across weeks, months, and years.

Most businesses treat the drip campaign as an afterthought: a series of promotional emails padded with occasional content. This approach produces list fatigue, declining engagement, and a subscriber base that slowly becomes indifferent to everything you send.

The Hero-driven drip campaign is built on a completely different philosophy: value is the point. The selling is the byproduct. Every email in the drip sequence should be something the reader is glad they received, regardless of whether they buy anything from it. The trust built by consistently delivering useful, honest, personality-driven content over time produces a level of commercial responsiveness that no single sales sequence can match.

Think about the newsletters, emails, or creators whose communications you look forward to. What makes them different from the ones you ignore? Almost certainly: they have a consistent voice, they say things you find useful or interesting, they treat you like an intelligent adult, and they don't feel like they are constantly trying to sell you something. That's the bar. That's what the Hero-driven drip campaign aspires to be, and the reason most business email falls so far short is that most businesses treat their list like a resource to extract from instead of an audience they're concerned about.

## Building the Drip: Structure and Pacing

A well-built drip campaign has three layers: the content layer, the trust layer, and the commercial layer. These layers don't occur in strict sequence. They weave through each email and across the campaign as a whole.

**The content layer** is the pure value. Specific knowledge that helps the reader make progress toward the thing they opted in to achieve. A tip they can implement today. A perspective that reframes something they were thinking about wrong. A case study showing how someone like them achieved something they want. A resource they didn't know existed. This is the Hero demonstrating expertise and investment in the reader's success with every send.

**The trust layer** is essentially the soul of the business, it's humanity. The origin story revisited, a mistake the Hero made and what they learned, a genuine opinion about something happening in the industry, a personal story that connects to the content topic, a moment of transparency that shows the Hero is a real person rather than a content machine. The trust layer is what separates a good email from a great one, because it's what makes the reader feel like they know you rather than just learning from you.

**The commercial layer** is the sales portion of the campaign. The mention of a product in the context of demonstrating how it helped someone. The link to a case study that happens to be about a specific offer. The periodic dedicated promotional email for a launch or a special offer. The commercial layer should never dominate the drip, I try to follow the three-to-one ratio (three value emails for every one commercial emphasis) as a guideline.

### The Drip Campaign Schedule: What It Looks Like

Here is a complete ninety-day drip campaign schedule for a home fitness coaching business, showing the Hero in action across ten emails. Notice the subject lines, the content types, the pacing, and where the commercial elements appear. This is the template you will adapt for your own business and your own Hero.

**90-DAY DRIP SCHEDULE — HOME FITNESS COACHING**

| Day | Subject Line | Type | Core Topic | CTA |
|---|---|---|---|---|
| 17 | The real reason most home workouts fail by week three | CONTENT | Common failure mode in home fitness, the boredom wall and how to design around it | None. Pure value |
| 21 | What I got wrong for the first two years of training at home | TRUST | Hero's personal story about a specific mistake: equipment over programming | None. Relationship building |

| 25 | The 20-minute workout that outperforms an hour in the gym | CONTENT | Specific workout methodology with explanation of the science | Download the printable version (free) |
|---|---|---|---|---|
| 29 | A reader asked me something I'd been avoiding | TRUST | Q&A format. Honest answer to a reader question about results timeline | Reply with your own question |
| 35 | She hadn't exercised in eleven years. Here's what happened. | PROOF | Client story. Specific results, specific timeline, specific obstacles overcome | See the full story (soft mention of program) |
| 41 | The equipment I use (and what I wasted money on) | CONTENT | Honest gear review. What matters and what is marketed nonsense | None |
| 48 | Why I built the program the way I did | TRUST | Behind-the-scenes of Hero's program design philosophy, connects to offer naturally | Learn more about the program (first soft offer) |
| 54 | Three nutrition mistakes that cancel out your training | CONTENT | Actionable tip: specific, implementable, useful | None. Pure value |

| | | | | |
|---|---|---|---|---|
| 60 | If you've been meaning to start, this is the reason | COMMERCIAL | Dedicated email for the program. Full offer, testimonials, deadline or availability | Enroll now (hard offer) |
| 67 | One thing before I change the subject | COMMERCIAL | Follow-up offer email. Handles one specific objection, simpler close | One more chance to join (last call) |
| 74 | The question everyone asks after the first month | CONTENT | Back to pure value: managing expectations, celebrating wins, building retention | None. Back to relationship mode |
| 88 | Something I've never written about publicly | TRUST | Deeper personal story. Builds the next layer of relationship before next commercial push | Reply if this resonates |
| 96 | The next phase. Here's what I'd do if I were starting today | CONTENT | Evergreen high-value piece. Foundational advice positioned as a gift | Download the guide (leads to new offer) |

## Reading the Schedule: What Each Email Is Doing

Look at the ratio in that schedule: eleven emails, eight of which have no direct commercial call to action. That's the ratio that builds a list that buys when you finally do make an offer. The two dedicated commercial emails on days sixty and sixty-seven arrive after forty-three days of consistent value and relationship building. By then, the reader isn't evaluating whether to trust you, that question was answered weeks ago, the only question now is whether the offer is right for them.

Notice also that the trust emails (the personal stories, the mistake admissions, the behind-the-scenes moments) aren't soft promotional content dressed up as vulnerability, they're genuine. The story about the wrong focus for the first two years is a real story. The Q-and-A is a real reader question. The trust layer works because it's true. Fabricated vulnerability does not build trust, it undermines it when the inconsistency becomes apparent.

Notice the subject lines. Not a single one says "Here is our newsletter" or "Weekly update from [Business Name]." Every subject line sounds like it came from a person who thought of the reader specifically and wrote them about something specific. That's what opens emails.

## Drip Schedules for Other Business Types

Here is a compressed view of the drip arc for each of the other business types, showing the first six emails after the welcome sequence ends. Adapt the structure to your Hero, your domain, and your specific offer.

**DRIP ARC — ARTISAN COFFEE SUBSCRIPTION**

| Day | Subject Line | Type | Core Topic |
|---|---|---|---|

| 17 | Why your coffee tastes different every morning (it's not the beans) | CONTENT | Water temperature and its outsized effect on extraction. Actionable fix |
|---|---|---|---|
| 21 | The worst coffee I ever tasted, and what I learned from it | TRUST | Hero's personal story about a specific bad experience and what it taught them |
| 27 | The region nobody talks about (but should) | CONTENT | Deep dive into an under-known coffee origin with flavor profile breakdown |
| 33 | A customer sent me this and I couldn't stop thinking about it | TRUST | Reader letter or DM that reflects the brand's values. Builds community feeling |
| 40 | What most coffee subscriptions get wrong | CONTENT | Hero's honest take on the subscription model and what makes one worth keeping |
| 47 | Your next shipment. What's coming and why I chose it | COMMERCIAL | Soft offer email. Next box preview doubles as a renewal/upgrade nudge |

## DRIP ARC — FREELANCE BUSINESS COURSE

| Day | Subject Line | Type | Core Topic |
|---|---|---|---|
| 17 | The email that got me my first $3,000 client (copied here exactly) | CONTENT | Annotated real outreach email. Shows the thinking behind each line |

| | | | |
|---|---|---|---|
| 21 | I almost quit freelancing in month four. Here's what stopped me. | TRUST | Hero's most difficult period. Honest and specific, no false resolution |
| 28 | Why freelancers undercharge (it's not what you think) | CONTENT | Psychological basis of underpricing. Reframes the problem and the solution |
| 35 | She went from $15/hour to $85/hour in six months. Here's how. | PROOF | Specific student result. Detailed, credible, inspiring, mentions the course once |
| 42 | The proposal mistake that's costing you clients right now | CONTENT | Specific tactical error in proposal writing with concrete fix |
| 50 | I want to share something I don't talk about publicly | TRUST | Deeper Hero story. The thing that nearly ended the business before it started |

## DRIP ARC — BOOKKEEPING FOR SMALL BUSINESSES

| Day | Subject Line | Type | Core Topic |
|---|---|---|---|
| 17 | The number most small business owners never look at (and should) | CONTENT | Gross margin vs. net margin. What it reveals and how to track it simply |
| 21 | What happened when I looked at my own books after six months away | TRUST | Hero's personal story of financial neglect and the wake-up moment |

| 28 | The tax deduction most solo operators miss every year | CONTENT | Specific, actionable, immediately valuable. Positions Hero as trusted advisor |
|---|---|---|---|
| 35 | A client almost made a $40,000 mistake. We caught it in time. | PROOF | Anonymized client story. Specific mistake, specific catch, specific outcome |
| 42 | Are your books ready for Q4? | CONTENT | Seasonal relevance. Actionable checklist framed as service to the reader |
| 50 | What clean books feel like (most people never find out) | COMMERCIAL | Soft offer. Emotional reframe of what good bookkeeping makes possible |

## Writing the Drip in Batches

The drip campaign is not a sprint. It is a long-running infrastructure project that you build over time, in batches, maintaining consistent quality across many months of content.

The approach that works: plan the full arc at a high level first (twelve to twenty-four months of email topics, scheduled at whatever cadence you have chosen: weekly, bi-weekly, twice-weekly). Do not try to write all of them at once. Instead, write in batches of five to eight emails every two to four weeks, staying four to six weeks ahead of the schedule. This gives you both the planning horizon to see the arc clearly and the flexibility to respond to timely topics when they arise.

Claude is a significant asset for the drafting phase of drip email production. You give it the topic, the trust or content angle, the voice reference, and any specific story or example you want it to use, and it produces a working draft. You then need to edit the draft to bring it fully into the Hero's voice, adding the specific details and personal observations that only you have. The combination of AI drafting speed and a few iterations of your edits will produce consistent, high-quality emails at a volume that would otherwise be unsustainable for a solo operator.

The one thing Claude cannot give you for the trust-layer emails is your actual stories. The mistakes you made, the moments that changed your thinking, the customer interactions that stayed with you. These need to come from your own experience. Make a practice of keeping a running list of these moments: not polished stories, just notes. "Client X said something that surprised me today." "Made a decision I regret about Y." "Realized something about Z while doing W." These notes become the raw material for your best trust-layer emails.

**✦ DRIP CAMPAIGN EMAIL PROMPT**

```
Write a drip campaign email for my business. Here is
everything you need:
HERO VOICE: [Paste your voice description from the Hero
Identity prompt, or describe it here]
EMAIL TYPE: [CONTENT / TRUST / PROOF / COMMERCIAL – choose
one]
TOPIC: [The specific topic this email covers]
RAW MATERIAL: [For TRUST emails: the actual story, in rough
```

```
notes. For CONTENT: the specific knowledge you want to
convey. For PROOF: the actual customer result. For
COMMERCIAL: the offer details.]
WHERE IN THE DRIP: [Approximate day number — this tells
Claude how warm the audience is and how much selling is
appropriate]
Write the complete email: - Subject line (2 options: one
that leads with curiosity, one that leads with the specific
value) - Preview text (the snippet that shows in the inbox
preview) - Full email body. Write in the Hero's voice, not
in a generic voice. This is a letter from a person to a
person. - Call to action (or explicit note that this email
has no CTA; pure value) - P.S. (always include; this gets
read almost as frequently as the subject line)
SPECIFIC INSTRUCTIONS FOR THIS TYPE OF EMAIL: - CONTENT:
Lead with the most useful thing, not with the framing. Give
something actionable in the first paragraph. - TRUST: Start
with the moment, not the lesson. Put the reader in the scene
first, then earn the reflection. - PROOF: Name the result in
the subject line. Prove it in the body. Do not oversell.
Specific details are more persuasive than enthusiasm. -
COMMERCIAL: Lead with something other than the pitch. Earn
the sales paragraph by giving value first, even briefly.
```

**Note:** *For trust emails, the raw material is the single most important input. A well-written trust email from a vague prompt produces a generic story that sounds invented. The same prompt with specific, real, rough notes (exact dialogue, specific timeline, actual details) produces something that reads unmistakably as true. Give Claude your actual notes, however messy.*

## The Difference Between a List and an Audience

There is a meaningful difference between having a list and having an audience, and the Hero-driven drip campaign is the marketing device that bridges the two.

A list is a set of email addresses — numbers in a database. It can be bought, rented, or scraped. It produces open rates and click rates and nothing else. When you sell to a list, you are broadcasting into a crowd of strangers.

An audience is a group of people you've nurtured and cultivated a relationship with who know who you are, who chose to hear from you, who have been shaped by consistent contact with your voice and point of view over time. When you sell to an audience, you're making an offer to people who already trust you. This changes the conversion math, the customer quality, and the long-term economics of the business in your favor.

The drip campaign, done the Hero way, transforms a list into an audience over twelve to eighteen months of consistent, genuine, valuable contact. The emails that go unread in month two are read reliably in month nine. The subscribers who are vaguely curious in month one are invested in month six. The relationship compounds, slowly and then faster, exactly the same way all real relationships do.

Build the Hero, build the drip, run it for two years without cutting corners, and at the end of that period you will have an asset that's harder to replicate than any single funnel or product launch you could ship in the meantime. Most businesses never get there because the timeline feels too long in month three. The ones that do are nearly impossible to dislodge once they've arrived.

# Chapter 11: The Strategic Brief You Can Write in an Afternoon

---

I'm not going to make you write a forty-page business plan. That document exists for bank loans and institutional investors, neither of which you need at this stage of the game.

What you do need is a one-page strategic brief, a clear, honest summary of what you're building, who you're building it for, how you plan to reach them, what you're going to charge, and whether the economics of it make any sense. Call it whatever you want, I call it the strategic brief.

It serves two purposes. First, it forces you to put every major decision in writing, which immediately reveals which ones you've thought through and which ones you've been vaguely hoping will work out. Second, it becomes your compass during execution, the document you come back to when you're deep in the weeds and need to remember what you're building and why.

Write it when the research and positioning work is done, then update it when something fundamental changes. Never let it get more than one page. The discipline of keeping it to one page forces you to prioritize what matters.

**✦ STRATEGIC BRIEF PROMPT**

```
I'm building a one-page strategic brief for my business.
Here's everything I've developed so far:
MARKET RESEARCH SUMMARY: [Paste your key findings – the pain
point, the opportunity, the market size estimate]
CUSTOMER AVATAR: [Your avatar description]
COMPETITIVE POSITION: [Your USP and positioning territory]
MY RESOURCES: [Be honest: budget, time per week, relevant
skills, existing audience if any, technical capabilities]
Please help me produce a concise strategic brief covering:
1. BUSINESS CONCEPT (1 paragraph): What the business is, who
it serves, what it does for them, and why it's worth
building.
2. REVENUE MODEL: Products/services, prices, and the
realistic path to first dollar, first $1,000 MRR, and first
$10,000 MRR. What are the assumptions driving these numbers?
3. CUSTOMER ACQUISITION PLAN: How do I get my first 100
customers? What channels, what lead generation hook, what
```

```
conversion path? What does acquisition cost look like at
each stage?
4. THE 90-DAY LAUNCH PLAN: If I can only do 5 things in the
first 90 days, what are they? List them in priority order
with specific deliverables for each.
5. KEY METRICS: What 4-5 numbers should I track weekly to
know if the business is working? (Not vanity metrics.
Actionable leading indicators that tell me whether I'm on
track.)
6. RISK MAP: What are the 3 most likely ways this fails?
What's the early warning sign of each, and what's the
response?
7. THE HONEST ASSESSMENT: Given everything above, is this a
compelling use of my time and resources for the next 12-24
months? What would need to be true for this to be a clear
yes?
Write this in plain language. No jargon. This is a document
I'll use, not a pitch deck.
```

**Note:** *The honest assessment question is the most important one. If you can't answer it with a clear yes, even a conditional yes with specific criteria, that's information. Not every business idea you research should become a business you build. Better to know now than six months in.*

## Planning Vs. Doing

The strategic brief is sufficient to stop planning and start building. I say this because smart, analytical people (the kind of people who read books like this) are prone to a specific failure mode: endless planning as a substitute for execution. Planning feels like progress. It's intellectually engaging, it doesn't involve risk, and you can always find one more thing to think through before you're ready. The strategic brief is done, and now you want to refine the avatar, and then you want to do more competitive research, and then you realize you should probably understand the SEO landscape better before you build...

At some point, the plan has to give way to action. The brief gives you enough to start. Real customers will teach you more than any amount of additional research. The first hundred people who interact with your funnel will tell you what's wrong with it in ways that no analysis could predict.

Use the brief as a starting hypothesis. Launch. Learn. Update the hypothesis. Build again. That is the actual process, and the brief isn't meant to eliminate the risk of launching. It's meant to make sure you're launching with the most important questions already answered, so the lessons you learn from real customers are the lessons only real customers can teach.

# Part Four: Funnels — Building Your Sales Infrastructure

---

# Chapter 12: Funnels — What They Are and Which Type to Build

The word "funnel" is everywhere in online business, and it carries enough jargon baggage that a lot of smart people tune it out. Let me strip away the jargon and say what a funnel actually is.

A funnel is a sequence. A series of steps that moves a stranger from first encountering you to becoming a paying customer — and ideally a repeat customer who refers others. It's called a funnel because the volume narrows at each step. Many people see your ad. Fewer click to your landing page. Fewer still opt in. Fewer still buy. Of those who buy, fewer still become the loyal customers who keep buying and tell their friends.

Your job is to design each step of that sequence to maximize the percentage of people who take the next step. The efficiency of each step — measured as a conversion rate — determines your economics. Improve the conversion rate at any step and you get more output from the same input. That's the leverage.

Without a funnel, you're leaving almost everything to chance. Someone finds your site, looks around, maybe sees a product they want, maybe figures out how to buy it, maybe does. A funnel replaces that chaos with a path — a deliberate sequence that does the selling for you, handles objections at the right moments, and guides the customer to the natural next action.

## The Stages of a Funnel

Every effective marketing funnel has five stages, even if the specific tactics within each stage vary widely from business to business. Awareness, Interest, Consideration, Decision, Retention and Expansion.

Awareness. Someone becomes aware that you exist. They see a social post, a search result, a YouTube video, an ad, a referral from a friend. This is the top of the funnel — the widest part, and typically the most expensive to fill.

Interest. The person does something to learn more. They click to your site, they follow you, they watch more of your content, they read your emails. They're evaluating whether you're worth more of their attention.

Consideration. They're actively thinking about whether what you offer solves their problem. They're reading your sales page, comparing you to alternatives, looking for social proof, reading your reviews. This is where persuasion does its heaviest lifting.

Decision. The moment of purchase. The mechanics of this stage — checkout page design, payment options, guarantee presentation, risk reversal — have an enormous impact on conversion rates.

Retention and expansion. What happens after the first purchase? Do they buy again? Do they upgrade? Do they refer friends? This is where most businesses leave the majority of their potential revenue unrealized.

Those five stages are universal. The specific tactics that serve each one — the pages, the offers, the emails, the automations — are what the rest of this section walks you through chapter by chapter.

## The Economics of Getting This Right

Let me put real numbers on what funnel thinking means for your business, because thinking about this in the abstract sometimes hides how meaningful the lift is.

Imagine you're driving 1,000 visitors to a single product page on your website. Your conversion rate is 1 percent — 10 sales at $97 each. Revenue: $970. Not terrible, not great. That's where most small businesses live, and most of them assume they need more traffic to make more money.

Now you build a proper funnel with the same traffic. A landing page with a compelling headline converts visitors to product page viewers at 40 percent. The product page, with better copy and stronger social proof, converts at 3 percent. An order bump on the checkout page is taken by 20 percent of buyers at $27. A one-click upsell after purchase is taken by 25 percent of buyers at $67.

Run the math. Four hundred of the thousand visitors reach the product page. Twelve of them buy, at $97 each

— that's $1,164 from the primary offer. Twelve buyers times a 20 percent bump take rate times $27 is another $65. Twelve times a 25 percent upsell take rate times $67 is another $201. Total revenue from the same 1,000 visitors: $1,430.

That's a 47 percent increase in revenue from the same traffic, just by building the right sequence rather than relying on a single sales page. And this is a conservative example. Well-optimized funnels regularly show 2x to 3x revenue improvements over unoptimized alternatives because the effect of small gains at each step compounds quickly.

Those improvements compound in another way too. More revenue per visitor means you can afford to pay more to acquire each visitor, which opens up traffic channels that were previously uneconomical, which scales the whole system. The business with the better funnel economics out-competes on advertising even when the product is similar, because the downstream revenue supports the investment. That's the actual leverage in this part of the book, not more traffic but better economics per visitor.

## How FunnelKit Pro Maps to the Five Stages

FunnelKit Pro is the tool this book recommends for building what we're describing. Here's how it handles each of the five stages.

The awareness and interest stages happen outside FunnelKit. Your ads, your content, your SEO, your social — those are the channels that fill the top of the funnel, and they're a different conversation. FunnelKit picks up the visitor at the consideration stage, when they land on your site. From that point forward it handles the entire sequence.

Opt-in pages capture interest and build your list. Sales pages do the heavy persuasive lift. Checkout pages — this is where FunnelKit's optimized checkout is a meaningful upgrade over stock WooCommerce — convert the decision. Order bumps at checkout and one-click upsells after purchase trigger the transaction-value lever from Chapter 8. Thank you pages extend the relationship into the retention stage. And FunnelKit Automations handles the email sequences that build on the first purchase — welcome flows, post-purchase nurture, win-back campaigns, abandoned cart recovery.

Every element in that stack gets its own chapter. The lead magnet funnel, the free-plus-shipping funnel, and the advanced funnel types all get their own section in this chapter, the copy that makes them all work in Chapter 13, and the upsell strategy in Chapter 14. This chapter gives you the map while those chapters give you the terrain.

### Where to Start — The Entry Point Question

The single most important architectural decision in your funnel is the entry point. Not the checkout page, not the upsell sequence, not the email automation — the entry point. What does the visitor see first?

The wrong entry point sabotages everything downstream. A visitor who lands on a hard-pitch sales page when they're not ready to buy bounces. A visitor who lands on a slow-rolling free lead magnet when they were ready to buy today feels patronized and goes to a competitor who's willing to sell them something. Matching the entry point to the traffic temperature is the architectural decision that determines whether anything else in the funnel matters.

Cold traffic — visitors who have never heard of you — almost always needs a softer entry point. A lead magnet that delivers immediate value. A free-plus-shipping offer that lets them sample the brand at minimal risk. A value-first piece of content that earns the opt-in. The sale comes later, once trust is built.

Warm traffic — visitors who already know you, your email list, your repeat site visitors, your social audience — can be taken to the offer directly. They've already done the relationship work. A sales page that gets straight to the offer outperforms a soft opt-in for this audience because making a warm buyer opt in again before you'll sell them anything is its own kind of friction.

Read the chapters that follow with the traffic temperature question in mind. The right entry point is the one that matches where your audience actually is, not the one that sounds most sophisticated.

**✦ FUNNEL ARCHITECTURE PROMPT**

```
I'm designing the funnel architecture for my business. I
don't need copy yet — I need the structural plan.
BUSINESS: [What you sell] MAIN PRODUCT: [The core offer and
its price] CUSTOMER AVATAR: [One paragraph — who they are,
what they want, what they've tried] EXISTING ASSETS: [List
size, audience, content, other products already available]
TRAFFIC SOURCE(S): [How traffic will come to this funnel —
paid ads, SEO, email, podcast guest appearances, referrals,
etc.] TRAFFIC TEMPERATURE: [Cold, warm, or mixed — and why]
Please design the complete funnel architecture:
1. ENTRY POINT: Given the traffic temperature, what's the
right first page — opt-in lead magnet, tripwire, direct
sales page, or free-plus- shipping offer? Defend the choice.
2. FUNNEL FLOW: Map every page in the sequence. What does
the visitor see first? What happens next? What happens after
they convert? Name each step and describe its job in one
sentence.
3. CORE OFFER STRUCTURE: At the point of sale, what's being
offered and at what price? Is it the main product, a
tripwire that leads to the main product, or a bundle?
4. ORDER BUMP: What specific product or service would work
as an order bump on the checkout page, and at what price?
Why is it a natural companion to the core offer?
5. ONE-CLICK UPSELL: After the primary purchase, what upsell
makes sense? What price, and what's the emotional logic for
why the buyer would take it in that moment of peak
commitment?
6. POST-PURCHASE EMAIL ARCHITECTURE: What automated email
sequence fires after purchase? How many emails, what's the
goal of each, and how does the sequence set up repeat
purchase?
7. EXPECTED ECONOMICS: Given reasonable conversion
assumptions for this type of funnel, what does the customer
economics look like? Initial average order value, expected
upsell lift, estimated lifetime value?
8. THE WEAK POINT: Of everything you've designed, which step
is the most uncertain — most likely to underperform and most
important to test first?
```

**Note:** *The structural plan comes before the copy. Don't ask Claude to write the headlines or the emails in this prompt — that work happens in the chapters that follow, once the architecture is right. Building copy before you've designed the funnel is how you end up with beautiful words that lead nowhere.*

## The Lead Magnet Funnel

**Lead Magnet Funnel — The Complete Flow**

Before you sell anything, you need a list.

I know that's not what you want to hear if you're eager to generate revenue. Building a list feels like doing setup work before the main event, but the email list is the main event, it’s the most valuable asset in your business, and getting to meaningful list size — people who know you, trust you, and have opted in to hear from you — is what makes everything else possible.

Every product launch I run performs dramatically better than it would with just cold traffic, because I'm launching to an audience that has been warming up for months or years. Every promotion I run gets a baseline of sales immediately from people who are already bought in. Every new relationship I build with the market starts with the credibility of an existing community rather than from scratch.

The lead magnet funnel is how you build that asset. It offers something valuable for free in exchange for an email address, and then delivers value through email that builds the relationship before you ask for anything.

## What Makes a Lead Magnet Work

Most lead magnets fail for three reasons, and they're all connected. They're not specific enough, not immediately valuable, or mismatched to the audience.

Not specific enough: '10 tips to get healthier' attracts nobody in particular. 'The 7-Day Gut Reset Protocol for Women Who've Tried Every Diet' attracts the exact right person. Specificity is what creates the 'that's for me' reaction. The more specific the lead magnet, the fewer people who opt in — and the more likely those people are to eventually buy.

Not immediately valuable: the person who opts in should get something they can use today. A checklist, a template, a quick-win guide, a protocol with specific instructions. If the value requires weeks of reading before anything useful happens, you'll lose people before the relationship starts.

Wrong audience match: the lead magnet needs to attract the same person who will eventually buy your main offer. I know this sounds obvious, but you would be surprised how it's regularly violated. The lead magnet about productivity hacks builds a list of productivity enthusiasts who are not necessarily interested in your fermentation kit. The magnet has to foreshadow and pre-sell the offer that follows.

**✦ LEAD MAGNET DESIGN PROMPT**

```
I need to design a high-converting lead magnet for my business. Here is the full context: BUSINESS: [What you sell]

CUSTOMER AVATAR: [Core pain, identity, what they desperately want]

MAIN OFFER: [What you eventually want them to buy – product, course, service, whatever]

MY EXPERTISE: [What do you specifically know that would be valuable to this customer?] Please help me design the ideal lead magnet: 1. LEAD MAGNET CONCEPTS: Generate 8 lead magnet ideas. For each, specify: - Format (checklist, short guide, template, email course, video, assessment, challenge, etc.) - Specific, compelling title – write the actual title, not a placeholder - The exact pain or desire it addresses - How it creates natural desire for the main offer - How quickly someone gets value from it (hours? days? immediately?) 2. SCORING: Rate each concept on: - Conversion potential (how excited would my avatar be to get this?) - Lead quality (how strongly does it signal likely interest in the main offer?) - Production cost (how hard is it to create and deliver?) 3. RECOMMENDED WINNER: Which lead magnet is the strongest choice and why? 4. TITLE OPTIMIZATION: For the winning concept, write 6 title variations testing different emotional angles: speed of result, specificity of outcome, identity alignment, fear of missing out, ease of implementation, curiosity. 5. CONTENT OUTLINE: Give me the full content outline – every section, every subsection, every key point I need to cover to deliver on the title's promise. 6. THE IMMEDIATE WIN: What specific, tangible thing can the person do or know in the first 10 minutes of consuming this lead magnet? That immediate win is what makes people love it and trust you.
```

**Note:** *After you choose your lead magnet concept, Claude can help you write the actual content. For a checklist or guide, give it the outline and ask it to write each section. For an email course, give it the topic for each email and ask it to draft the sequence. The content creation goes much faster when the strategic design work is done first.*

### The Landing Page

Your lead magnet needs a dedicated landing page — a single, focused page with one purpose: collect the email address. No navigation links. No sidebar. No other offers. One page, one action.

The elements of a converting opt-in landing page are simple: a headline that states the transformation, a subheadline that adds specificity, three to five bullet points that describe the specific value the person gets, some form of social proof if you have it, and the opt-in form with a button that says something more compelling than 'Submit.'

That button copy matters more than most people realize. Research consistently shows that buttons stating what the person gets outperform buttons stating what they do. 'Send Me the Protocol' outperforms 'Download.' 'Get My Free Guide' outperforms 'Subscribe.' The button copy should complete the sentence 'Yes, I want to...'

**✦ LEAD MAGNET LANDING PAGE PROMPT**

```
Write the complete copy for my lead magnet landing page.
Here's everything: LEAD MAGNET: [Name and 2-sentence
description]

CUSTOMER AVATAR: [Core pain, exact language they use, what
success looks like to them]

BRAND VOICE: [Describe your voice — formal or casual,
specific phrases, anything that characterizes it]

SOCIAL PROOF: [Any testimonials, number of previous
subscribers, notable mentions — or 'none yet'] Please write:
1. HEADLINE (3 variations): State the transformation. Be
specific. Speak to the pain or the desire. These should be
compelling enough that someone who sees them immediately
knows whether this is for them. 2. SUBHEADLINE: One sentence
```

```
that adds specificity to the headline — 'who it's for' or
'how fast' or 'even if you've tried before' 3. BULLET POINTS
(5): Each bullet describes one specific thing they get from
the lead magnet. Format: benefit statement, not feature
statement. 'How to X so you can Y' rather than 'includes
information about X.' 4. SOCIAL PROOF ELEMENT: Either use
what I have, or if I have nothing, write a 'join N others
who have' statement I can update when real numbers exist. 5.
BUTTON COPY (4 variations): Complete the sentence 'Yes, I
want to...' — should be specific, action-oriented, and match
what the person is excited to get. 6. BELOW-FORM LINE: One
sentence that addresses the spam/unsubscribe fear. Should be
reassuring without sounding like a legal disclaimer. 7. PAGE
HEADLINE FOR THE BROWSER TAB: Short and specific. Write
everything in my brand voice. This is a conversation with
one specific person, not a broadcast to a demographic.
```

**Note:** *Build this page in FunnelKit Pro. For step-by-step instructions on creating opt-in pages, configuring the form, and connecting it to your email platform, refer to the official FunnelKit documentation at funnelkit.com.*

## The Thank You Page and First Impression

After someone opts in, where do you send them? Most businesses send them to a boring confirmation page that says 'thanks, check your email.' This is a waste of the most engaged moment in the entire customer relationship.

The person who just opted in is as warm as they're going to be until they've consumed your content and bought something. Their interest is at its peak. They've just raised their hand and said 'I want what you're offering.' Use this moment.

A good thank you page does three things: confirms they made the right decision, introduces you as a human being they want to know, and sets clear expectations for what's coming via email. If the economics support it, you can also present a low-friction first offer — a tripwire product priced at $7 to $27 — that takes advantage of the buying-adjacent mindset.

Even without a paid offer, write a genuine personal introduction on the thank you page. Three paragraphs. Tell them who you are, why you created this lead magnet, and what they can expect from your emails. This is your first impression, make a good one. Make them feel like they've just met a person, not opted into another marketing list.

## The Free-Plus-Shipping Funnel

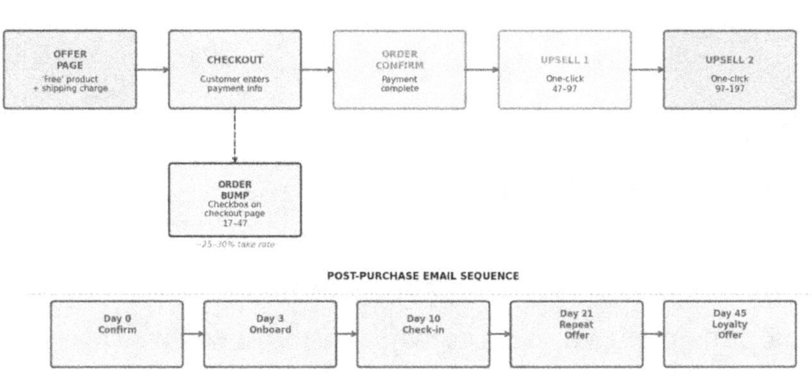


The free plus shipping model has been a staple of direct response marketing for decades, and it works for a simple, durable reason: the word 'free' is the most powerful word in consumer psychology.

The mechanics are simple. You offer a physical product at no cost to the customer, asking them to pay only for shipping and handling. The shipping charge — typically $5.95 to $9.95 — covers or nearly covers your actual fulfillment cost. You acquire a customer for little or no net cost on the front end.

What makes this model so strategically valuable is not the initial transaction — it's what it proves. Every person who fills out their payment information to claim a free-plus-shipping offer has demonstrated three things: they want what you're offering, they're willing to take an action to get it, and they have an active payment method they're willing to use. That's a dramatically stronger signal than an email sign-up, and it opens up a relationship that's measurably more valuable commercially.

## The Economics That Make It Work

The free plus shipping model only works if your back-end monetization is strong enough to make the economics positive. Let me walk through the math.

Say your free product costs $4 to produce and $3.50 to ship. Your shipping charge is $7.95. You net $0.45 on the initial transaction. That's not a business — that's barely breaking even. The model works because of what comes after.

On the checkout page, you offer an order bump — a complementary product priced at $17 to $37. If twenty-five percent of customers take it, you're now making about $5 per customer on average from the bump alone. Immediately after checkout, a one-click upsell offers a related product at $47 to $97. If twenty percent take it, you're now at roughly $15 to $25 net per customer.

Then the email sequence starts. You have a customer who has given you their physical address and payment information. You know what they're interested in — they proved it by breaking out their credit card. You have a warm list of people who have bought from you. The backend email sequence, promoting related products over the following weeks and months is where the mathematics of the model starts to get interesting.

Average customer lifetime value in a well-run free plus shipping funnel is often five to fifteen times the initial shipping charge. The front-end economics are break-even or near it. Maximizing the lifetime value is the business we're building.

**✦ FREE PLUS SHIPPING OFFER DESIGN PROMPT**

```
I want to design a free plus shipping customer acquisition
funnel. Here's my business context: BUSINESS: [What you
sell]

CUSTOMER AVATAR: [Core pain and desire]

EXISTING PRODUCTS: [What you already have or could offer as
```

```
the free item]

MAIN BACKEND OFFER: [What you want customers to eventually
buy] Please help me design this funnel: 1. FREE PRODUCT
SELECTION: What physical product should be the free offer?
It should: be valuable and exciting to my avatar, be small
and light for low shipping cost, be producible or sourceable
at under $5-6, and naturally create desire for my backend
product. Give me 3 candidates with production/sourcing
notes. 2. FUNNEL ECONOMICS: For the best candidate, walk me
through: - Estimated production cost per unit - Estimated
fulfillment/shipping cost - Optimal shipping charge to break
even or near it - What order bump take rate and price do I
need to be net positive on acquisition? - What backend
sequence revenue do I need to build a real business? 3.
OFFER PAGE COPY: - Headline for the free offer page (3
variations) - 3-4 bullet points that make the free offer
feel irresistibly valuable - Trust/credibility element for
the page 4. ORDER BUMP: What complementary product should
appear on the checkout page? Give me: the product, the price
point, a one-sentence description, and the specific headline
for the bump box. 5. ONE-CLICK UPSELL: What product should
fire immediately after payment? Give me: the product, the
price, the emotional angle of the pitch, and the key reason
to take it now vs. later. 6. POST-PURCHASE EMAIL SEQUENCE
STRUCTURE: Outline the first 7 emails after someone claims
the free offer. For each email: timing, purpose, and core
content. Think about this as designing the full customer
relationship, not just the initial transaction.
```

**Note:** *The back-end email sequence is where this model makes money. If you design the front-end funnel without planning the email sequence that follows it, you've built an expensive lead generation system with no monetization. Plan both together.*

## Advanced Funnel Types

The lead magnet funnel and the free plus shipping funnel will cover most of your needs at the early stages. But the funnel landscape is richer, and as your business grows, you'll want to add additional funnel types for specific purposes. Here's a working overview of the other major types, with enough detail to know when each is right.

### The Tripwire Funnel

A tripwire is a low-priced offer — typically $7 to $37 — made immediately after an opt-in. The name comes from the idea that once someone crosses the line from non-buyer to buyer, even at a trivial price, something fundamental changes in the relationship. They've proven to both you and themselves that they are willing to buy from you.

The conversion logic here is well-documented — people who have bought from you at any price are dramatically more likely to buy from you again than people who have never bought. A tripwire converts a subscriber into a customer — and customers have measurably higher lifetime value and responsiveness than subscribers.

The tripwire product needs to feel like a legitimate bargain at the stated price. Not a cheap thing priced cheaply. A real thing of obvious value steeply discounted as an explicit introduction offer that tells the customer 'I want you to experience what I do before you commit to the full thing'. This framing is honest, and customers respond to it.

### The Webinar Funnel

For products priced above $500 — courses, coaching programs, consulting, high-ticket services — the webinar funnel is often the most effective conversion mechanism available. It gives you 60 to 90 minutes to demonstrate your expertise, to build a genuine relationship with the audience, to deliver real value, and to make an offer to a highly engaged audience.

Here's how it works. Traffic hits a registration page. Registration kicks off a pre-webinar email sequence that builds anticipation and gets people to actually show up. The webinar runs live, delivers content, and ends with an offer. A post-webinar sequence picks up the people who didn't buy during the live event.

If you do it right webinars convert at rates that are hard to match with written sales pages alone because they create a live, interactive relationship. Done poorly — thin content padding a long pitch — they permanently damage trust. The ratio that works seems to be seventy to seventy-five percent genuine value, twenty-five to thirty percent offer.

Claude can help you design the webinar content, write the registration page, and script the follow-up sequence. The webinar itself — your presence, your expertise, your stories, your conviction — that's you. No AI replaces it.

### The Challenge Funnel

The challenge funnel combines lead generation with an immersive experience that builds genuine results before the sale. A five-day challenge invites participants into a short structured experience with daily actions toward a specific outcome.

The challenge funnel is powerful for a specific reason: by day five, participants have done real work, achieved small wins, built a relationship with your teaching, and experienced a version of the transformation your main product promises. The conversion that follows is not a stranger buying from a marketer — it's someone who has just worked with you for five days deciding to go deeper.

Challenge conversion rates can be extraordinary, twenty to thirty percent of active participants, because the qualification and relationship-building happen during the challenge itself.

The overhead is real, though. Challenges require daily live or recorded content, active community management during the five days, and a strong offer ready at the end. They're worth building, though, when you have an established audience and a high-ticket offer to sell.

### The Application Funnel

For high-touch, high-price services, coaching at $3,000 and above, consulting, done-for-you services, the application funnel reverses the normal dynamic. Instead of persuading people to work with you, you set up a process where they apply to work with you, and you decide whether to accept them.

The application itself is the conversion mechanism. When someone fills out an application describing their situation, goals, and what they've already tried, they make the case for themselves. By the time you get on a call with them, they're already invested in working with you, the application process has done this work for you.

The application funnel also creates a perception of selectivity which is really valuable for premium positioning. You've changed the paradigm — you're not selling, you're qualifying. This dynamic shift changes everything about the sales conversation.

## Choosing Where to Start

The right first funnel depends on your situation. If you have nothing — no audience, no list, no proof of concept — start with the lead magnet funnel. Build your list first. Everything is easier with a list.

If you have a physical product business and want to build customer acquisition at low cost, the free plus shipping funnel is your move. If you have a high-ticket offer and an existing audience, consider a webinar or a challenge. If you're selling services or coaching, consider the application funnel.

In every case: start with one funnel, build it properly, and optimize it before adding complexity. A single well-executed funnel outperforms three half-built ones every time.

# Chapter 13: Writing Copy That Sells Without Sounding Like Copy

---

Forty years of writing direct response copy taught me one thing above everything else — the headline is not decoration. The headline IS the ad. Everything beneath it either capitalizes on the attention the headline captured or it fails to sustain interest.

I have written headlines for television spots that had to do their work in the first three seconds before a viewer reached for the remote. I have written direct mail packages where the outer envelope headline determined whether the entire piece went in the trash or got opened. I have seen headline changes double response rates on campaigns that had run for years. The headline is not a creative exercise, it's a commercial decision with a measurable consequence. Think of the micro-second you have to grab someone's attention — that's the heavy lifting your headline needs to do.

Digital copy is no different. The mechanics of the screen are different from the mechanics of the television spot or the direct mail package, but what drives a human being to read rather than scroll, to click rather than leave, to buy rather than hesitate — that hasn't changed. I have watched digital copy fail for the same reasons direct mail copy failed in 1987, and I've watched it work for the same reasons.

What follows is how to write funnel copy that converts, not copy that wins awards or impresses other marketers. I'm singularly focused on copy that moves product — there's a difference.

Funnel copy is a specific genre with specific jobs to do at each stage. It's different from brand copy, which builds awareness and identity over time. Funnel copy has to do all of its persuasion work in a single encounter — often with a stranger who found you through a search or an ad and has no existing relationship with your brand.

That's a harder job than most people appreciate. You have a few seconds to establish relevance, a few more to establish credibility, a few more to articulate the problem so well that the person feels understood, and then you have to design and present an offer that makes the decision to act feel obvious.

Every element of funnel copy has a job. The headline's job is to get the subheadline read. The subheadline's job is to get the body copy read. The body copy's job is to build desire and handle objections. The CTA's job is to translate that desire into action. Nothing is decorative, every word should serve a purpose.

## The Architecture of a Converting Sales Page

A long-form sales page follows a structure that has been refined over decades of direct response marketing. The order matters because it mirrors the psychological sequence a prospect goes through when making a considered buying decision.

Headline: The single most important element. It has to capture the big promise in a way that immediately signals relevance to the right reader.

Opening story or hook: Establishes emotional connection. Makes the reader feel understood rather than sold to. The best openings say, implicitly, 'I know exactly what you're dealing with because I've been there too.'

Problem statement: Articulates the problem in the reader's own language with enough specificity and emotional accuracy that they nod along. This is where your customer avatar research pays off directly.

Agitation: Deepens the pain before you offer the relief. What does it cost them financially, emotionally, in their relationships — to leave this problem unsolved? This is not manipulation, it's about helping them understand why acting is important.

Solution introduction: The bridge from problem to offer. Why does a solution exist, and why is this the right one?

Offer presentation: What exactly is included, why it's valuable, how it works.

Social proof: Evidence that the promise is real — testimonials, case studies, results.

Value stack: The full offer presented as a package, with individual values that make the asking price feel like a bargain.

Guarantee: Risk reversal. The stronger and more specific, the better.

Call to action: Clear, specific, action-oriented.

**✦ SALES PAGE COPY PROMPT**

```
Write a complete long-form sales page for my offer. Here is
everything you need: OFFER: [Name and full description of
exactly what you're selling]

PRICE: [The asking price]

CORE PROMISE: [The single most compelling transformation
this delivers]

CUSTOMER AVATAR: [Full description – their pain, their
failed attempts, their exact language, their desires, their
identity, their objections]

VALUE STACK: [List everything included and what you'd
normally charge for each element]

GUARANTEE: [Your risk reversal – the stronger and more
specific, the better]

SOCIAL PROOF: [Testimonials, results, relevant credentials –
or 'placeholder needed' if you don't have them yet]

BRAND VOICE: [How you talk – casual, expert, personal,
direct, any specific things you always or never say] Write a
complete sales page in this structure: 1. HEADLINE +
SUBHEADLINE: The big promise. Specific. Speak directly to
the transformation. Three headline options. 2. OPENING
(paragraphs 1-3): Meet the reader exactly where they are.
Acknowledge the problem and the emotional weight of it. Make
them feel understood before you sell them anything. 3.
PROBLEM AGITATION (paragraphs 4-6): Deepen the pain. What
does it cost them to leave this unsolved? What is the true
price of staying where they are? Use their language, not
marketing language. 4. POSITION SHIFT (paragraph 7): There
is another way. Bridge from the problem to the possibility
of the solution. 5. SOLUTION INTRODUCTION (paragraphs 8-10):
Introduce yourself and your offer. Why you? What makes your
approach different? Tell the story of how you developed
this. 6. WHAT YOU GET: Present the full offer as a
```

```
narrative, not a list. Build excitement. Each element should
add to the sense that this is exactly what they need. 7.
SOCIAL PROOF SECTION: Real testimonials (or convincing
placeholders) with specific outcomes. 8. VALUE STACK:
Present all included items with values. Build to the total,
then reveal the price as a fraction of the total. 9.
GUARANTEE: State it simply and confidently. The strength of
the guarantee should signal the strength of the product. 10.
FINAL CLOSE: One more picture of the transformation. Then
the clear, specific CTA. Write in my voice. Personal, not
corporate. One specific person reading this should feel it
was written for them.
```

**Note:** *Long-form sales pages feel excessive until you understand their purpose: they're answering every question a serious buyer might have so that by the end, the only reason not to buy is that you don't want the thing. Short pages leave objections unanswered. Answered objections convert.*

# Chapter 14: The Upsell Math — How Order Bumps and Upsells Double Your Profit Per Customer

---

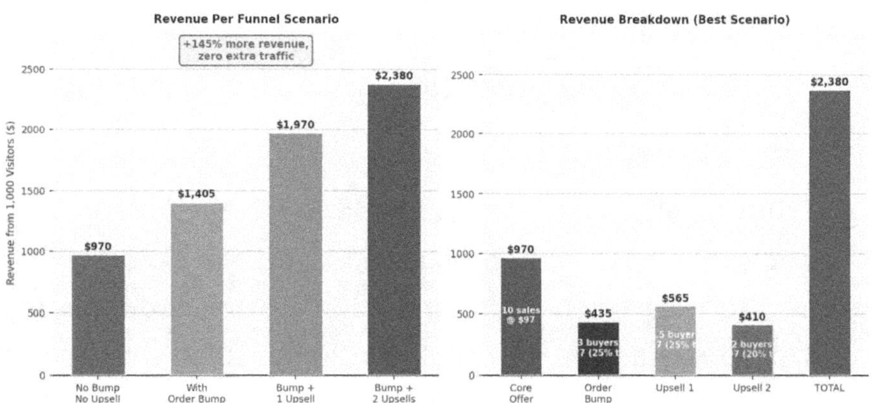


I am going to be direct with you about something that most people dancing around this topic never come out and say: if you are running a funnel without an order bump and at least one upsell, you are leaving roughly thirty to sixty percent of your potential revenue on the table. Every single day. On traffic you already paid for.

That is a conservative estimate based on real funnel data across thousands of businesses. The math of bumps and upsells is so clear, and the mechanics are so straightforward to implement, that there is no excuse for not having them. Once you understand what the numbers look like before and after, you will never build another funnel without them.

### The Baseline — A Funnel Without Bumps or Upsells

Let's build a realistic baseline scenario. You are selling a core offer at $97. You drive 1,000 visitors to your funnel. A well-optimized funnel converts at about one to two percent of cold traffic — let's use a solid one percent, which gives you ten sales.

Ten sales at $97 each: $970 in revenue from 1,000 visitors.

Now think about what you paid to get those 1,000 visitors. If you are running paid ads, you are likely paying somewhere between $0.80 and $2.50 per click depending on your niche and platform. At $1.20 per click, you spent $1,200 to generate $970 in revenue. You just lost $230.

This is the core problem with single-product funnels at cold traffic: the economics rarely work. The customer acquisition cost exceeds the revenue from a single transaction, and you are dependent entirely on the hope that customers buy again later to make the math positive. Some will, but you have no control over when and no strategy to capture value from the buying mindset they are in right now, while they are at the moment of peak purchase intent.

The order bump and the upsell are the mechanisms that fix this. Not by getting more traffic and not by improving your conversion rate (which is hard and slow), but by extracting more revenue from the customers you are already converting at the moment they are already in a buying mindset.

### The Order Bump — The Checkbox That Changes the Math

An order bump is a single additional offer presented on the checkout page itself, typically as a checkbox with a short description. The customer does not need to re-enter their payment information. They check a box, and the item is added to their order. That's the entire mechanic.

The psychological reason it works so well is the customer has already made the decision to buy. The buying decision is the primary psychological barrier — the willingness to hand over payment information and commit — and in this instant that barrier is gone. They are in a yes-state. Adding something relevant and modestly priced to that yes-state is a significantly easier ask than the original sale.

Order bumps typically convert at twenty to thirty percent of buyers. That means for every ten people who purchase your core offer, two or three will add the bump. At a bump price of $27, that adds $54 to $81 to your revenue from ten sales — a revenue increase of five to eight percent from a checkbox. At a bump price of $47, $94 to $141 added.

The order bump should be something that directly complements the core offer and enhances the result the customer is about to get. It should be something the customer would obviously want alongside what they just bought. It should be priced low enough that the buyer says yes without thinking, and it should be something you can deliver digitally or package without significant additional fulfillment cost.

### Order Bump Examples by Business Type

Here is how order bumps work across five different business types. Notice that in every case, the bump is a natural companion to the core offer — not a random upsell, but something the customer would obviously want alongside what they are already getting.

Home fitness coaching. Core offer: a twelve-week home workout program at $97. Order bump: a customized weekly meal plan and grocery guide at $27. Why it works: someone buying a workout program is already thinking about getting healthier and the meal plan is the obvious missing piece.

Artisan coffee subscription. Core offer: a three-bag sampler box at $49. Order bump: a fourth bag of the most popular coffee in the box at $16. Why it works: the buyer has already decided they want coffee from this roaster. The fourth bag is the easiest yes in the world.

Freelance business course. Core offer: a thirty-day course on landing freelance clients at $197. Order bump: a swipe file of fifty email and proposal templates at $47. Why it works: the course teaches the strategy. The templates are the execution tools. The customer needs both so offering them separately at checkout is doing the customer a service.

Local landscaping business. Core offer: a premium lawn care annual contract at $899. Order bump: a spring aeration and overseeding service for one flat fee of $149. Why it works: the customer already values their lawn enough to pay $899 annually and aeration is the obvious professional add-on.

Bookkeeping for small businesses. Core offer: monthly bookkeeping service at $349 per month. Order bump: a one-time business financial audit and setup call at $97. Why it works: a new bookkeeping client has messy books and they know it. The audit call fixes the foundation and makes the ongoing service more effective.

### The One-Click Upsell — Revenue After the Sale

The one-click upsell fires immediately after the checkout is complete. The customer has paid. They are on the confirmation page. They see a new offer, and because their payment information is already in the system, they can accept it with a single click — no forms, no re-entry, just yes or no.

This is the most important mechanic to understand: the upsell is not a second attempt to sell them something they were not willing to buy. It is an upgrade or expansion of the decision they just made. They bought the workout program. Now they are offered the private coaching add-on. They bought the coffee sampler. Now they are offered a three-month subscription. They bought the freelance course. Now they are offered a done-for-you proposal review session. The upsell should feel like the natural next step on the same journey, not a separate pitch.

One-click upsells typically convert at fifteen to twenty-five percent. At $67 per upsell and a twenty percent take rate, that adds $134 in revenue from ten sales. Add a second upsell at $97 with a fifteen percent take rate on those who accepted the first, and you add another $29 in revenue per ten sales. These numbers compound quickly.

## The Full Math — Before and After

Now let's run the complete comparison. Same 1,000 visitors. Same one percent conversion rate on the core offer. Same $97 core product.

Without bumps or upsells: Ten sales at $97 equals $970.

With an order bump at $27 and a twenty-five percent take rate: $970 plus 2.5 sales at $27 equals $970 plus $67.50 equals $1,037.50.

Add a first upsell at $67 and a twenty percent take rate: plus 2 sales at $67 equals another $134. Running total: $1,171.50.

Add a second upsell at $97 and a fifteen percent take rate on the 2 who took the first upsell: plus 0.3 additional sales at $97. Running total approximately $1,200.

That is a twenty-four percent revenue increase from the same traffic. Your average order value went from $97 to approximately $120. Your customer acquisition cost stayed the same. Your cost to deliver likely increased slightly, but for digital products, minimally.

Now look at the paid traffic math. At $1.20 per click for 1,000 visitors, you spent $1,200. Without bumps and upsells, you generated $970 — a $230 loss. With bumps and upsells, you generated approximately $1,200 — breakeven. And breakeven on cold traffic means your backend email sequence, your repeat purchase emails, your cross-sell campaigns — all of which is now pure profit. The customer was acquired at cost. Everything after the first transaction is margin.

That is why bumps and upsells are not optional extras. They are the mechanism that makes paid traffic viable.

## Upsell Examples by Business Type

Home fitness coaching. First upsell after buying the workout program: a monthly virtual check-in call with a coach, $47 per month. Second upsell: access to a private community of program members, $19 per month. Both are recurring revenue additions on a one-time purchase.

Artisan coffee subscription. First upsell after buying the sampler: upgrade to a six-month subscription with fifteen percent off each box, billed monthly at $42. The customer just demonstrated they like the coffee. The subscription is the obvious logical extension. Second upsell: add a curated brewing equipment bundle at $89, one-time.

Freelance business course. First upsell: a live group Q-and-A session plus thirty-day private community access, $97. Second upsell: a personal portfolio and LinkedIn review session with the instructor, $147. Both deliver value the course itself does not — direct access to the teacher.

Local landscaping. First upsell after signing the annual contract: priority scheduling guarantee ensuring same-week service for any issues, $199 per season. Second upsell: bi-annual tree and shrub deep feeding treatment, $249 per visit. Both are things a lawn-focused customer obviously wants.

Bookkeeping service. First upsell: a quarterly business performance review call with the bookkeeper to discuss the numbers, $197 per quarter. Second upsell:

payroll processing add-on, $79 per month. Both are natural extensions of the accounting relationship already established.

## Downsells — Catching People Who Say No

When a customer declines an upsell, the funnel does not have to end there. A downsell is a reduced version of the declined offer, presented immediately after the decline. If they said no to the $97 coaching call, present a $47 group workshop on the same topic. If they said no to the six-month subscription, offer a single extra box at ten percent off. Not everyone who declines the full offer is uninterested — some are price-sensitive at that moment.

Downsells convert at lower rates than upsells — typically five to twelve percent — but they recover revenue that would otherwise be zero and they can do so without damaging the relationship if handled right. The framing matters enormously. The downsell should never feel like desperation or like you are cheapening what you just offered. It should feel like a genuine alternative that serves a different need at a different investment level.

Not every funnel needs a downsell. If your upsell is already modestly priced and well-positioned, a downsell may add complexity without meaningfully adding revenue. Build your bump and upsell sequence first. Add downsells only when you have data showing significant upsell decline rates and you have a compelling reduced offer to present.

### ✦ BUMP AND UPSELL SEQUENCE DESIGN PROMPT

```
Design a complete order bump and upsell sequence for my
funnel. Here is my full context: CORE OFFER: [Name,
description, and price of what you are selling]

CUSTOMER AVATAR: [Who they are, what they just bought, what
they want to accomplish]

MY ADDITIONAL PRODUCTS OR SERVICES: [Everything else you
offer that could be presented as a bump or upsell]

CONSTRAINTS: [Digital-only delivery? Service capacity
limits? Anything that affects what you can offer?] Please
design: 1. ORDER BUMP: - The specific product or service to
offer as the bump - The optimal price point and reasoning -
The exact two-sentence description that appears on the
checkout page - The headline for the bump box - Why this
bump is a natural companion to the core offer - Realistic
expected take rate and revenue math 2. UPSELL 1 (fires
immediately after checkout): - The product or service -
Price and reasoning - The core emotional argument for
accepting it now rather than later - The specific headline
and opening line for the upsell page - Realistic take rate
and revenue math 3. UPSELL 2 (fires after Upsell 1, whether
accepted or declined): - The product or service - Price and
positioning - How this differs from Upsell 1 in what it
offers - Realistic take rate and revenue math 4. DOWNSELL
(optional – fires after declining Upsell 1): - Is a downsell
appropriate here? If not, explain why. - If yes: what is it,
at what price, and how is it framed? 5. FULL REVENUE MODEL:
Show me the before-and-after math. Assume 1,000 funnel
visitors, a realistic conversion rate for my offer type, and
the take rates you recommended. What does revenue look like
with and without this sequence? What does the average order
value change to? 6. THE PRESENTATION TEST: Read back the
complete sequence as if you were a customer moving through
it. Does it feel like a natural progression of one purchase
decision, or does it feel like being sold to repeatedly?
What adjustments would make it feel more natural?
```

**Note:** *The presentation test question is the one most builders skip. A bump and upsell sequence that feels like a barrage of additional sales pitches damages the customer relationship and increases refund rates. The sequence should feel like obvious opportunities the customer is glad to know about, not a gauntlet they have to survive.*

# Part Five: Email — Building Relationships at Scale

# Chapter 15: Why Email Still Works

---

Every year or two, someone writes a think piece declaring that email is dead. The thesis is usually the same: young people don't use email, social media is where attention lives now, email open rates are declining, chatbots are going to replace it.

Every year or two, the data says the same thing back: email is not dead. It has an average return of $36 to $42 for every dollar spent — a figure that has been consistently reported by multiple major industry analyses across more than a decade. No other marketing channel is even close.

I want to explain why, because understanding why email works helps you use it better.

## The Ownership Argument

The most important thing about your email list is that you own it.

Your Instagram following doesn't belong to you — it belongs to Meta. They can change the algorithm, throttle your reach, ban your account, or shut down entirely. All of these things have happened to real businesses. The businesses that were built entirely on social media audiences have faced repeated existential crises every time the platforms changed the rules.

Your email list is yours. You have the list of addresses. You own the relationship. Nobody can change the rules on how many of your subscribers receive your messages. When you press send, your email goes to the inbox of every person on your list.

This is not a small thing. It is the fundamental reason to prioritize list building over social following building, especially in the early stages of a business. A social following has value, but an email list has permanence.

### The Intent Signal

The second reason email works is that everyone on your list took an active step to get there.

Social media followers happen passively — someone sees your content, taps follow, and forgets about it. Email subscribers made a decision. They saw your lead magnet, decided it was worth their email address, went through the opt-in process then confirmed their subscription. That's five or six friction points, each of which required a conscious affirmative action.

People who do that are different from passive followers. They're telling you they want what you have. They're raising their hand. The email list is a list of people who have explicitly said 'I want to hear from you.'

That's the best possible audience for your marketing messages.

### The Relationship Argument

The third reason email works is that it's a personal medium. Email arrives in the same inbox as messages from your mother, your boss, and your friends. The social contract of email is intimate in a way that social media is not.

When you send an email that sounds personal, specific, and genuine — not like a broadcast, but like a letter — it lands differently. The best email marketers I've observed write emails that read like personal correspondence rather than marketing communications. The emails feel like they came from a person who thought of you specifically, not a list manager who pressed send.

Claude helps you write emails at this level of quality because it can iterate on voice and specificity in a way that doesn't require you to be a professional writer. The output needs editing and refinement to get fully into your voice — but the gap between a good Claude draft and a publishable email is much smaller than the gap between a blank page and a publishable email.

Build the list. Protect the list. Send emails worth reading. That's the whole discipline of email marketing, and it's what the next three chapters are about.

◆ **Email is where the One-Person Marketing Department does its best long-term work. No face, no team, no agency relationship. Just a consistent voice and a systematic approach to building trust over time.**

## Chapter 16: Email Sequences — The Welcome and What Comes After

---

The welcome sequence is the most important thing you will ever write for your business. I know that's a strong statement. I mean it.

In direct response television, we called the first sixty seconds the hook. Everything before the viewer decided to keep watching or change the channel. Fortunes were made and lost on those sixty seconds. The copy, the production values, the offer structure — all of it was in service of keeping that viewer engaged long enough to get to the phone number.

Your welcome sequence is the same sixty seconds, stretched across five to seven emails. Your subscriber just opted in. They're as warm as they'll ever be until they've bought something. They have a vague memory of you and a specific reason they joined — whatever you offered them. The welcome sequence is your chance to convert that vague memory into a real relationship, and that specific reason into a deep understanding of everything you offer.

I have seen businesses with mediocre products succeed because their welcome sequence was extraordinary. I have seen businesses with excellent products fail because they thought the product would sell itself and skipped the relationship-building work. The product doesn't sell itself, the relationship sells the product and the welcome sequence builds that relationship.

The welcome sequence is the most important set of emails you will ever write. It arrives when subscriber engagement is at its absolute peak — immediately after they opt in, when your name is fresh and their interest is high. Open rates on welcome sequences are often two to three times higher than ongoing broadcast emails. Click rates are higher. Conversion rates are higher.

You will never again have your subscriber's attention at this level until they've bought something from you and you're doing post-purchase follow-up. The welcome sequence is your one chance to set the foundation for everything that follows.

Getting it right means: delivering what you promised, establishing your voice and personality, building genuine credibility, and creating a relationship that makes people look forward to your next email.

Getting it wrong means a list full of people who have mentally unsubscribed even if they haven't technically unsubscribed yet. They're there, but they're not really there.

## The Architecture of a Welcome Sequence

A solid welcome sequence for most businesses runs five to seven emails over the first ten to fourteen days. Here's the structure that works, and why each email does what it does.

Email 1, Day 0: Delivery and introduction. Deliver what you promised — the lead magnet, the guide, the discount code, whatever they opted in to get. Then introduce yourself briefly and genuinely. Not your credentials — you. Who you are, why you built this, what you care about. Close by setting expectations: here's what's coming in your inbox over the next couple of weeks.

Email 2, Day 2: Your story. The deeper version of who you are and why you do this. Tell the origin story — how you got into this, what led you here, what you've learned and struggled with and discovered. Stories build trust faster than any other format. People who understand where you came from are much more loyal than people who only know what you sell.

Email 3, Day 4: Pure value, no pitch. Give them something useful — a specific tip they can apply today, a shortcut that solves a real problem, a perspective that reframes something they've been thinking about wrong. No CTA to buy anything. Just "here's something valuable from me to you because I care about your success." This email is important because it proves you're not just here to sell to them.

Email 4, Day 7: Social proof and credibility. Results, testimonials, case studies, notable endorsements. This email builds the confidence that what you do works before you ask for anything. Done right it won't feel like bragging, it will feel like evidence that you can deliver on the relationship you've been building.

Email 5, Day 10: The first offer. A soft introduction to your main product or an appropriate entry offer. Don't lead with the sale, lead with the natural next step in the relationship you've been building. 'If you found the last four emails valuable, here's the thing I built for people who want to go deeper...'

Email 6, Day 13: Follow-up on the offer. Address the objections you know exist. Add a testimonial that speaks to a specific hesitation. If there's a deadline, remind them. Make the case one more time from a different angle.

Email 7, Day 16: Transition email. You're transitioning from the intense welcome sequence into the ongoing nurture. Tell them what kind of emails they'll receive going forward, how often, and what value those emails will deliver. This manages expectations and reduces future unsubscribes.

**✦ WELCOME SEQUENCE PROMPT**

```
Write a complete 7-email welcome sequence for my business.
Here's everything you need: BUSINESS: [What you sell]

LEAD MAGNET: [What they opted in to receive]

CUSTOMER AVATAR: [Core pain, desires, language, what they
```

```
care about]

MY STORY: [The real story – how you got into this, what
you've learned, what drives you. The more specific and real,
the better.]

FIRST OFFER: [What you want to introduce at Email 5 –
product, price, what it does]

BRAND VOICE: [Describe your voice. Include specific things
you always say, things you never say, your register, your
personality] For each of the 7 emails, write the COMPLETE
EMAIL:

- Day/timing

- Subject line (2 options – one straightforward, one
curiosity-based)

- Preview text

- Full email body

- CTA

- P.S. (always include a P.S. – it gets read nearly as often
as the subject line, and it's prime real estate for urgency,
a personal note, or a detail that didn't fit the body)
Sequence arc:

- Emails 1-3: Deliver value, establish who you are, build
trust

- Email 4: Evidence and credibility

- Emails 5-6: Natural introduction of the offer with full
handling of objections

- Email 7: Transition into ongoing relationship Apply the
Strategy of Preeminence throughout: position the sender as
the trusted advisor who is invested in the reader's success,
not the vendor who wants to close a sale. These emails
should feel like letters from a knowledgeable friend, not a
marketing sequence. Write all 7 emails in full. Do not
summarize or outline – write the actual email content.
```

**Note:** *After Claude writes the sequence, read it out loud. Every email. The ones that sound like marketing copy rather than conversation — fix them. The test: would you send this email to one specific person you care about? If the answer is no, it needs work.*

## Voice Consistency Across the Sequence

The most common problem with welcome sequences written with AI help is voice inconsistency. Email three sounds like one person, email five sounds like a different person.

The fix: edit every email against a specific voice reference before you publish it. Your voice reference is a few hundred words from writing you've done yourself — a real email you sent, a post you wrote, anything that sounds like you. Keep that reference open while you edit the AI-generated drafts.

Specifically, look for: sentences that are too long and complex for your natural voice, words you would never use, hedging or qualification you wouldn't add, structural moves (like bullet points) that feel out of character, and sign-offs or transitions that sound corporate rather than personal.

The goal is not for every email to be identical in tone — you're different in different moods, and that variation is fine and welcome. The goal is for each email to sound unmistakably like you.

## Ongoing Email Automation

After the welcome sequence wraps up — usually around day seventeen to twenty — your subscriber enters what most email systems call the regular nurture flow.

This is the ongoing communication that maintains and deepens the relationship over months and years.

There are two types of emails in the long-term system: drip sequences (automated, triggered by time or behavior) and broadcasts (sent manually when you have something specific to say). You need both, and they serve different functions.

### Drip Sequences

Drip sequences are automated emails that fire on a schedule after the welcome sequence ends. Think of them as a long-running educational and relationship-building program that runs in the background regardless of what you're actively doing in the business.

A good drip sequence has a theme for each email — a specific piece of your expertise, a story, a tip, a piece of content that's useful to your avatar. It's not a series of promotions. It's a series of valuable encounters with your voice and thinking, peppered with the occasional soft offer or mention of your product.

The ratio I aim for: three to four value emails for every direct sales email. Most drip sequence emails can reference your products as natural teaching examples without feeling promotional. When you mention 'this is the approach I teach in [product],' you're providing context, not making a sales pitch. Reserve hard promotional emails — where the entire message focuses on driving a purchase — for your strongest offers.

**✦ DRIP SEQUENCE DESIGN PROMPT**

```
I need to design a 90-day drip email sequence for
subscribers after they complete my welcome sequence. Here's
the context: BUSINESS: [What you do]

SUBSCRIBER PROFILE: [Who is on your list, what they care
about, what they're trying to achieve]

MY EXPERTISE AND CONTENT: [What topics do you know well
enough to write valuable emails about? What stories, tips,
frameworks, or resources do you have to share?]

PRODUCTS TO REFERENCE: [What can you naturally mention or
promote in these emails?]

FREQUENCY: [How often will you email – once a week? twice a
month?]

VOICE: [Describe your email voice] Please design a 90-day
drip sequence plan: 1. CONTENT THEMES: Identify 6-8 major
content themes for the 90-day period. Each theme should
serve your audience and naturally connect to your products.
2. EMAIL CALENDAR: Map out every email in the 90-day
sequence by week. For each email: - Timing (day) - Content
theme - Email topic and angle - Type: Educational / Story /
Resource / Soft mention / Promotional - Subject line concept
3. PROMOTIONAL PLACEMENT: Where in the 90 days do you place
the 3-4 promotional emails? What product does each promote?
What's the angle for each promotion? 4. EVERGREEN PILLARS:
Which 5 emails in this sequence are so good that every new
subscriber should receive them? These are your 'greatest
hits' – the emails that best express your voice, deliver the
most value, and build the strongest relationship. 5. WRITE
THE FIRST 5 EMAILS IN FULL: Take the first 5 emails from the
calendar and write them completely – subject line, preview
text, full body, P.S. The goal: a subscriber who completes
this 90-day sequence should feel like they know you well,
trust your expertise, and have been helped by being on your
list.
```

**Note:** *Don't try to write the whole 90-day sequence in one session. Design the calendar first, then write emails in batches — maybe five at a time. Give yourself permission to build this over several weeks. A complete sequence is infinitely more valuable than a perfect email with nothing following it.*

## Broadcast Emails

Broadcast emails are the ones you write and send when you have something specific to say: a product launch, a promotion, a piece of content you're excited about, a timely observation that connects to your audience's life.

These are the emails that generate the most immediate revenue, because they're written with a specific purpose and a clear call to action. A good launch sequence of five to seven emails can generate more revenue in five days than your automated sequences generate in a month.

The rules for broadcast emails are simpler than welcome and drip sequences, but they matter. One big idea per email, one thing you want the reader to think, feel, or do. Multiple CTAs, multiple points, multiple offers — these will all reduce performance. One idea executed with conviction outperforms five ideas half-executed every time.

Use subject lines that pull their weight and earn the open. Your subscriber's inbox is full of emails competing for the same attention — your subject line has to create enough curiosity, promise enough value, or feel personal enough that they open yours. Test different subject line approaches and pay attention to what works for your specific audience.

A real hook that doesn't start with 'I hope this finds you well.' That phrase is the kiss of death for email engagement. Start with a story, a surprising observation, a question, a specific thing that happened. Get to the point fast and respect the reader's time.

**✦ BROADCAST EMAIL PROMPT**

```
Write a broadcast email to my list. Here's what I need:
AUDIENCE: [Who is on your list – your avatar]

PURPOSE: [What this email needs to accomplish – announce,
sell, educate, re-engage, share?]

THE MAIN THING: [The specific news, offer, story, or insight
which the core of this email]

BRAND VOICE: [Your voice description]

CALL TO ACTION: [What one thing do you want people to do
after reading?] Write a complete broadcast email that: 1.
Opens with a HOOK in the first 2 sentences – a story, a
surprising observation, a question, a specific scenario. NOT
'I wanted to share' or 'I hope you're doing well.' 2. Builds
naturally from the hook to the main point. The connection
should feel organic and earned, not mechanical. 3. Makes the
main point or offer clearly and with genuine conviction. 4.
Ends with ONE clear, specific call to action. The action
should be framed as a benefit, not a request. 5. Includes a
P.S. that adds something – urgency, an additional insight, a
personal note, a practical detail. The P.S. gets read almost
as frequently as the headline; don't waste it. ALSO WRITE:

- 3 subject line options: one curiosity-based, one value-
based, one conversational/personal

- Preview text for each subject line (the snippet that shows
in the inbox preview) Tone: written by a person who gives a
damn about the reader, not produced by marketing software.

Length: the shortest version that accomplishes the goal –
cut anything that doesn't do specific work.
```

**Note:** *After Claude drafts the email, read it immediately. Ask yourself: would I open this if I received it? Would I read it to the end? Would I click? Be honest. If the answer to any of those is no, identify specifically what's wrong and give Claude that feedback. The second draft is almost always significantly better.*

# Chapter 17: Tagging and Segmentation

---

## What Tags Are (And Why They Matter More Than You Think)

Tags are the invisible system that remembers everything your subscribers do, tracks where they are in your sales process, and determines which emails they receive next. Without proper tagging, your automations are just fancy broadcast emails. With smart tagging, they become intelligent systems that respond to behavior and guide people toward purchase.

A tag is a label that gets attached to a subscriber's profile. Think of tags as digital Post-it notes that record what people have done, where they came from, what they're interested in, and where they are in your sales process. When someone downloads your lead magnet, they get tagged "Downloaded: Profit Guide". When they click your pricing link, they get tagged "Interest: Pricing". When they purchase, they get tagged "Customer: Paid" and you remove "Prospect". Your email platform uses these tags to decide who gets what emails when.

Here's why this matters: without tags, you're sending the same emails to everyone. The person who just found you gets the same message as someone who's been following you for six months. The person actively shopping for your service gets the same email as someone who just wanted your free guide. That isn't marketing, that's spam with good intentions.

## The Five Essential Tag Categories

Every business needs these five types of tags. Start with these, then add others as your system grows.

### 1. Source Tags (Where They Came From)

- "Source: Facebook Ad" — they came from social media advertising
- "Source: Google Search" — they found you organically
- "Source: Referral" — someone sent them to you
- "Source: Webinar" — they signed up during a presentation

### 2. Interest Tags (What They Want)

- "Interest: Pricing" — they clicked your pricing page
- "Interest: Case Studies" — they want proof before buying
- "Interest: Enterprise" — they need larger-scale solutions
- "Interest: DIY Solution" — they want to do it themselves

### 3. Status Tags (Where They Are in Your Process)

- "Status: Prospect" — not a customer yet
- "Status: Customer" — has purchased
- "Status: VIP" — high-value customer

- "Status: Unengaged" — hasn't opened emails in 30+ days
- "Status: Hot Lead" — very engaged, likely to buy soon

#### 4. Action Tags (What They've Done)

- "Downloaded: Lead Magnet" — completed your opt-in
- "Attended: Webinar" — showed up to your presentation
- "Clicked: Book Call" — interested in speaking with you
- "Purchased: Product A" — bought your specific offering

#### 5. Sequence Tags (Which Emails They're Getting)

- "Sequence: Welcome" — in your new subscriber sequence
- "Sequence: Sales" — actively being pitched
- "Sequence: Nurture" — getting educational content
- "Sequence: Onboarding" — learning to use what they bought

## How Tags Make Your Automation Intelligent

Here's a real example of how tags create intelligent automation.

#### Sarah's Journey Through Your Funnel

- **Day 1:** Sarah downloads your lead magnet from a Facebook ad.

**Tags added:** "Source: Facebook", "Downloaded: Lead Magnet", "Status: Prospect", "Sequence: Welcome".

- **Day 3:** Sarah clicks the link to your case studies page in Welcome Email #2.

  **Tags updated:** Add "Interest: Case Studies". Upgrade "Status: Prospect" to "Status: Hot Lead".

- **Day 5:** Because Sarah has "Interest: Case Studies" plus "Hot Lead", she moves from the welcome sequence to the sales sequence.

  **Tags updated:** Remove "Sequence: Welcome". Add "Sequence: Sales".

- **Day 7:** Sarah clicks your pricing link and spends five-plus minutes on the page.

  **Tags added:** "Interest: Pricing", "Clicked: Pricing Page".

- **Day 8:** Because Sarah has "Interest: Pricing" plus "Hot Lead", she gets a personalized email with a limited-time discount.

  **No tag changes.** Sarah is now receiving tailored sales content that matches what she's shown interest in.

- **Day 9:** Sarah purchases.

  **Tags updated:** Remove "Status: Prospect" and "Sequence: Sales". Add "Status: Customer", "Purchased: Main Product", and "Sequence: Onboarding".

Without tags, Sarah would have gotten the same generic welcome emails as someone who never engaged.

With tags, she got a sequence that responded to her actual behavior and guided her toward the purchase she was already moving toward.

## Where to Add Tags in Your Automation Workflow

Tags should be added at every significant interaction point. Here's your checklist for when to apply them.

### When Someone Joins Your List

- Add a source tag (where they came from).
- Add an action tag (what they downloaded).
- Add a status tag ("Prospect").
- Add a sequence tag ("Welcome").

### When Someone Clicks a Link

- Add an interest tag based on what they clicked.
- Update status tag if warranted ("Hot Lead").
- Consider a sequence change based on interest level.

### When Someone Purchases

- Remove "Prospect" status tag.
- Add "Customer" status tag.
- Add the specific product purchase tag.
- Remove them from sales sequences.
- Add them to the customer onboarding sequence.

## How to Set Up Tags in FunnelKit

Here's exactly how to implement tagging in FunnelKit, with specific click-by-click instructions.

### Setting Up Tags on Opt-in Forms

**Step 1.** In your WordPress admin, go to FunnelKit → Funnels → [Your Funnel].

**Step 2.** Click "Edit" on your opt-in page.

**Step 3.** Click on your opt-in form to select it.

**Step 4.** In the left sidebar, look for "Actions" or "Form Settings."

**Step 5.** Find the "Tags" field and enter your tags separated by commas. Example: "Source: Facebook, Downloaded: Lead Magnet, Status: Prospect, Sequence: Welcome."

### Adding Tags Based on Link Clicks

**Step 1.** Go to FunnelKit → Automations → Create New Automation.

**Step 2.** Choose trigger "Link Clicked" from the list.

**Step 3.** Enter the specific URL you want to track (e.g., your pricing page URL).

**Step 4.** Click the "+" button to add an action.

**Step 5.** Choose "Add Tag" from the actions list.

**Step 6.** Enter the tag you want to add: "Interest: Pricing."

### Managing Tags When Someone Purchases

**Step 1.** Create a new automation with trigger "Order Completed."

**Step 2.** Add action "Remove Tag" → "Status: Prospect."

**Step 3.** Add action "Add Tag" → "Status: Customer."

**Step 4.** Add action "Add Tag" → "Purchased: [Product Name]."

**Step 5.** Add action "Remove Tag" → "Sequence: Sales." This stops sales emails.

## A Tag Naming Convention That Prevents Chaos

Here's how to name your tags so you can find them six months from now.

### Good Tag Names (Clear and Organized)

- "Source: Facebook Ad" (category: type)
- "Interest: Enterprise Sales" (category: type)
- "Status: Hot Lead" (category: type)
- "Purchased: Coaching Program" (category: specific product)

### Bad Tag Names (Confusing and Useless)

- "Facebook" (too vague)
- "Hot" (unclear what this means)
- "January 2024 Promo Clicked" (too specific, won't age well)
- "Customer New" (grammatically awkward)

## Why You Shouldn't Overdo Tagging

More tags aren't automatically better. Here's when to stop.

- Don't tag every page visit. Track meaningful actions only, like pricing page visits or case study downloads.
- Don't create tags you won't use. If you're not going to send different emails to people tagged "Clicked: About Page," don't track it.
- Don't over-segment. Having 47 different micro-audiences means you're writing 47 different email sequences.
- Don't forget to clean house. If you haven't used a tag in six months, delete it.

The goal is intelligent automation that serves your business, not a complex system that impresses other marketers. Start with the five essential categories, add tags only when you have a specific use for them, and clean house regularly.

With proper tagging, your email automation stops being a broadcast system and becomes a personalized sales assistant that knows exactly where each prospect is in your process and what they need to hear next.

## Segmentation

Email is powerful. Segmented email is dramatically more powerful.

Segmentation is the practice of dividing your list into sub-groups based on what you know about them — what they've purchased, what content they've engaged with, how recently they joined, what lead magnet they used to opt in, what demographic category they fit — and sending different messages to different groups based on that knowledge.

The business case for segmentation is relevance. An email that's highly relevant to the specific person reading it converts at a fundamentally higher rate than a broadcast to everyone on your list. When you send a 'we just launched a beginner fermentation kit' email to a segment of people who have already bought three products from you and are clearly advanced, that email is actively damaging the relationship. They feel like you don't know them.

When you send the same launch email to the segment of people who just joined your list through a 'fermentation basics' lead magnet, who have opened every email in your welcome sequence and clicked on the beginner content, but haven't bought anything yet — that email lands perfectly. It's the right offer to the right person at the right moment.

## The Segments That Matter Most

You don't need twenty segments. You need the segments that meaningfully change what you should say and how you should say it. Here are the five that matter most for most businesses at the stage this book is aimed at.

1. Buyers versus non-buyers. This is the most fundamental segment. Buyers have crossed the trust threshold. They've given you money. They already know you can deliver. Non-buyers are still evaluating. The messages appropriate for each group are completely different — buyers should be nurtured toward repeat purchase, non-buyers toward first purchase.

2. Engaged versus disengaged. Engaged subscribers open your emails regularly and click your links. Disengaged subscribers are technically on your list but haven't meaningfully interacted in months. Sending the same emails to both groups burns your deliverability (email providers notice when large portions of your list never engage) and your relationship with the engaged group by diluting the signal. The engaged group gets your best content and your best offers. The disengaged group gets re-engagement campaigns.

3. By lead magnet or entry point. If someone joined your list through a 'weight loss after 40' lead magnet, they told you something specific about what they want. If someone else joined through a 'strength training fundamentals' lead magnet, they told you something different. These two people are on the same list but have different needs, and a business sophisticated enough to acknowledge that will convert significantly better on relevant offers.

4. By purchase history. Past purchases reveal future buying intent and product needs. Customers who've bought your entry-level product are ready for upsell offers. Customers who've invested in your premium products are ideal candidates for advanced or complementary offerings. Non-buyers need low-risk entry offers that remove barriers to their first purchase. Target based on what they've already demonstrated they value.

5. By recency. A subscriber who joined last week is different from one who joined two years ago. A customer who bought last month is different from one who hasn't bought in a year. Recency is a strong signal of engagement and purchasing probability, and your messaging should reflect it.

## Building Segmentation Without Overcomplicating It

The mistake most businesses make with segmentation is trying to build an elaborate taxonomy before they have enough data or list size to justify it. You don't need thirty segments when you have a two-hundred-person list. You need buyers versus non-buyers, and engaged versus disengaged. That's it.

As your list grows and your business develops, you add segmentation layers when you have a specific, current reason for them. You build the 'recent buyer' segment when you have a post-purchase nurture sequence you want to run. You build the 'lead magnet X' segment when you have a product that's specifically relevant to people who came through that magnet. You build segments to serve a specific communication purpose — not speculatively.

FunnelKit handles behavioral segmentation natively, tagging customers based on their actions: which products they've bought, which funnels they've gone through, which automations they've triggered. Your email platform handles list-based segmentation based on opt-in source and engagement data. Between the two, you have everything you need to build a segmented communication architecture that's significantly more effective than mass broadcasting.

**✦ EMAIL SEGMENTATION STRATEGY PROMPT**

```
I want to build a smart email segmentation strategy for my business. Context: BUSINESS: [What you sell]

LIST SIZE: [Current subscriber count]

SEGMENT DATA I HAVE: [What do you know about your subscribers? Purchase history? Lead magnet source? Engagement data? Tags?]

EMAIL PLATFORM: [What platform are you using?] Please help
```

```
me design a segmentation strategy: 1. PRIORITY SEGMENTS:
Given my list size and available data, what are the 3-5 most
important segments to create first? For each: how to define
it, how to tag or identify who's in it, and what different
message they should receive. 2. SEGMENTATION MATRIX: Build a
simple matrix showing: for each segment, what is the primary
communication goal (first purchase? repeat purchase? re-
engagement? upgrade?), what offer is most relevant, and what
tone/approach is appropriate. 3. PERSONALIZATION
OPPORTUNITIES: What specific personalization can I add to my
existing emails that would make them feel more relevant to
specific segments? (Not just 'Hello {{name}}' – meaningful
personalization based on behavior or status.) 4. SEQUENCING
PLAN: What should happen automatically when someone moves
from one segment to another? (When a non-buyer becomes a
buyer – what fires? When an engaged subscriber goes inactive
– what fires?) 5. MEASUREMENT: How will I know if segmented
communication is working better than mass communication?
What metrics should I track for each segment?
```

**Note:** *Start with the buyer/non-buyer segmentation if you have nothing else in place. That single segmentation change — sending different messages to people who have and haven't bought — will improve your results immediately and visibly.*

# Part Six: Irresistible Offers — Creating Offers That Convert

---

# Chapter 18: The Five Elements of an Irresistible Offer

---

Offer design is where most businesses lose money they don't know they're losing. I spent years working on offers for some of the most competitive direct response categories there are — cellular service, satellite television, merchandise sold in ninety-second television spots to an audience that had one hand on the remote. In those environments, a weak offer didn't produce disappointing results, it produced nothing. The phone didn't ring, the website didn't convert — the silence was immediate and unmistakable.

That kind of accountability changes how you think about offers. You stop thinking about what sounds good and start thinking about what makes the decision easy. You stop trying to be clever and start trying to be clear, asking the question that separates a mediocre offer from an irresistible one — "does this make the customer feel that saying yes is obviously smarter than saying no?"

When the answer to that question is yes — when the value is undeniable and the risk is removed and the reason to act now is real — things convert at rates that feel almost shocking. I have watched the same product go from struggling to sell to generating thousands of orders simply by redesigning the offer around that single question. Not a different product, a different offer.

That's what this section is about.

There's a difference between a product and an offer. Most people who struggle to convert leads into customers have a product problem, not a marketing problem — but the product problem is often just an offer design problem.

A product is a thing: a course, a kit, a service, a membership. An offer is how you present that thing: the framing, the context, the value stack, the pricing structure, the guarantee, the bonuses that remove objections, the urgency that makes acting now feel better than waiting.

You can have a great product wrapped in a mediocre offer and struggle. You can have a mediocre product wrapped in a great offer and succeed for a while (eventually reputation catches up). What you want is close to unstoppable — a great product wrapped in a great offer.

This chapter is about building the offer side of that equation. The product side is up to you.

## The Five Elements of an Irresistible Offer

Every irresistible offer has five elements. When all five are present and well-executed, the decision to buy feels obvious to the right customer.

Element one: A specific, compelling core promise. Not 'you'll learn about email marketing' and not 'improve your results' — a specific, vivid, believable promise of what will change in the customer's life. 'By day thirty you'll have a complete email welcome sequence set up, running, and converting — or your money back.' That's a promise — specific, verifiable, and bold.

Element two: A value stack that makes the price feel small. The principle is simple: the total perceived value of everything included should be dramatically higher than the asking price. Not ten percent higher — four, five, ten times higher. When the math is obvious in the customer's favor, the decision becomes easy.

Element three: Targeted bonuses that neutralize the main objections. Every buyer has specific fears and hesitations. The bonuses that work best address those fears directly. If the main objection is 'this seems complicated,' the most valuable bonus is a quick-start guide that removes the complication. If the objection is 'I've tried things like this before and they didn't work,' the most valuable bonus is a coaching call or a diagnostic tool that ensures they don't make the same mistakes.

Element four: Risk reversal that makes saying no feel riskier than saying yes. A strong guarantee removes the financial risk from the equation. The customer's remaining risk is: will this work for me? The guarantee answers: 'if it doesn't, you lose nothing.' When you've removed the financial risk and the emotional risk, what's left to say no to?

Element five: Honest urgency or scarcity. A reason to act now rather than later. This can be a real deadline (the offer is only available at this price for a limited time), real scarcity (only fifty units available), or a natural consequence (if you don't start this process now, you're another month behind on building your list). The urgency must be real. Manufactured scarcity that the customer sees through destroys trust permanently.

**✦ IRRESISTIBLE OFFER DESIGN PROMPT**

```
I need to design a complete, irresistible offer for my
business. Here is all my context: CORE PRODUCT: [Full
description — what it is, what it does, how it works, what
transformation it delivers]

PRICE TARGET: [What price are you aiming for?]

CUSTOMER AVATAR: [Their pain, their objections, their
desires, their language]

COMPETITIVE CONTEXT: [What alternatives exist? What are they
missing that mine delivers?]

MY ASSETS: [What else do I have — templates, tools, access,
knowledge — that could be incorporated as bonuses?] Build me
a complete offer design: 1. CORE PROMISE: Write the
specific, testable promise of this offer. Not vague —
specific. What will have changed in the customer's life by a
defined point if they complete the program/use the product?
Write 3 versions at different boldness levels. 2. VALUE
STACK: - Core product with a legitimate value assignment -
4-5 bonuses, each chosen to address a specific objection or
desire - For each bonus: what it is, why it's valuable,
which specific objection or desire it addresses, suggested
value - Total stack value - Price reveal with ratio
calculation 3. GUARANTEE DESIGN: Write a specific risk
reversal that would make a skeptical, once-burned customer
feel that buying is safer than not buying. The guarantee
should: be specific (not 'satisfaction guarantee' but
exactly what you'll do), be time-bounded, reflect genuine
confidence in the product. 4. URGENCY/SCARCITY: What
legitimate reason exists to act now? Identify the real
urgency element available for this offer (NOT manufactured).
5. OFFER NAME: Give the full package a name that speaks to
the transformation rather than the product. 5 name options.
6. THE IRRESISTIBILITY AUDIT: Reading back this complete
```

```
offer – core promise, value stack, bonuses, guarantee, price
– what's still missing or weak? What would the most
skeptical member of my target audience say is not enough? 7.
THE 'WOULD YOU BUY IT?' TEST: If this offer was presented to
you and you were the target customer, would you buy it? Why
or why not? What would need to change?
```

**Note:** *The 'Would You Buy It?' test at the end is the most important part. If Claude reads back the offer and says it's compelling but not irresistible, push for specifics. Ask: 'What is the single change that would make this feel like an obvious yes?' Then make that change.*

## Risk Reversal — Going Further Than You're Comfortable With

I want to spend extra time on risk reversal because it's the element most businesses underinvest in.

The most effective direct response is 'risk reversal' at its extreme: taking all the risk of the purchase off the buyer and onto yourself. A standard money-back guarantee takes some risk off. A guarantee like 'If you complete the program and don't achieve this specific result, I'll refund you and let you keep the materials' takes almost all of it off.

If you believe in your product or service, don't be afraid of a strong guarantee. Most businesses worry about being taken advantage of, about someone asking for a refund after consuming all the content. While these fears are understandable, in practice they are largely unfounded.

The businesses that offer the strongest guarantees report the lowest refund rates. This isn't because they attract more ethical customers but because the strength of the guarantee signals that the business has genuine confidence in its product, which attracts customers who have genuine motivation to get results, who use the product properly, who get results, and who therefore don't ask for refunds.

The guarantee that makes you uncomfortable to offer is usually the guarantee that would most significantly move your conversion rates. Offer the guarantee you're afraid to offer, deliver an excellent product, and watch what happens.

# Chapter 19: Pricing Psychology — What You Know vs. What the Market Decides

---

The most common pricing mistake among new business owners is not charging too much — it's charging too little. The second most common pricing mistake is having no idea why they chose the price they did.

Pricing is not a guess. It's not 'what feels comfortable' or 'what I'd pay for this myself' or 'what competitors charge.' It's a strategic decision that reflects the value you deliver, the position you want to occupy in the market, the quality of customer you want to attract, and the economics required to build a real business.

When I finally understood pricing as a strategic lever rather than an awkward necessity, my business changed significantly. Not because I started charging more across the board — because I started charging with intention, for reasons I could articulate, and communicating those reasons to customers in a way that made the price feel obviously right.

## Value-Based Pricing in Practice

The correct way to price anything is from the customer's perspective: what is this result worth to them?

If you're selling a course that helps business owners stop wasting four hours a week on a specific administrative task, and the average business owner values their time at $100 an hour, you're delivering four hundred dollars of value per week — over $20,000 per year. Pricing the course at $997 is a screaming deal. The math is simple and the customer can do it themselves.

That's the exercise. Identify the specific value — in time saved, money earned, money not wasted, stress reduced, outcome achieved — and price your offer at a fraction of that value. The fraction should be large enough that the price feels significant (trivial prices signal trivial value) but small enough that the math obviously favors the customer.

Most people skip this exercise and instead look at what competitors charge, adjust slightly, and call it pricing. This approach leaves money on the table if you're better than the competitors, and positions you in a price race that nobody wins.

### The Price-Quality Perception

A well-documented psychological phenomenon is that in most markets higher prices are perceived as indicating higher quality. This is not irrational, price really is often a signal of quality, and people have learned to use it as such. The result is that, contrary to intuition, raising prices can actually increase conversion rates because the higher price triggers the 'this must be good' inference.

In markets where quality is hard to evaluate before purchase — which describes most information products, services, and many physical goods — price is one of the few available quality signals. A $97 course and a $997 course on the same topic send dramatically different signals about the depth, quality, and results of the content, even before the customer looks at any other information.

This doesn't mean charge as much as possible regardless of value delivered. It means you shouldn't be afraid to charge prices that reflect the actual value of what you do. The discomfort of charging high prices is usually about your own insecurity about whether you deserve the money, not about what the market will bear.

**✦ PRICING STRATEGY PROMPT**

```
I need to develop a pricing strategy for my business. Here
is the context: PRODUCT/SERVICE: [Full description]

CUSTOMER: [Avatar – their financial situation, what they
typically spend in this category, what price signals mean to
them]

COMPETITIVE LANDSCAPE: [What competitors charge – cheapest,
median, most expensive options]

VALUE DELIVERED: [What specific, measurable outcomes does
the customer get? Put numbers on time saved, money made, or
problem cost if solved vs. unsolved]

MY GOALS: [Revenue target, positioning aspiration, type of
customer I want to work with] Please build a complete
```

```
pricing analysis: 1. VALUE CALCULATION: What is the
specific, quantifiable value the customer receives if this
product delivers on its promise? Show the math – time saved,
money earned, cost of problem left unsolved. What does a
conservative, base, and generous estimate of total value
look like? 2. PRICING ARCHITECTURE: Design a three-tier
structure: - Entry tier: What's the right entry point for
first-time buyers? What's included? What price? - Core tier:
Where most customers should land. What's included? What
price? - Premium tier: Maximum support version. What's
included? What price? For each tier: justify the pricing
relative to the value delivered. 3. PRICE ANCHORING: How
does the premium tier anchor the core tier? Is the premium
priced high enough to make the core feel like a natural
choice? 4. PSYCHOLOGICAL PRICE POINTS: For my specific
product and customer, which psychological price points
matter? Is $97 vs $100 relevant here? When does charm
pricing help vs. harm premium positioning? 5. FIRST YEAR
ECONOMICS: At these prices, with realistic conversion rate
assumptions, what does first-year revenue look like at 3
customer volume levels: conservative, base, optimistic? 6.
THE INTEGRITY CHECK: Are these prices a genuine, fair
exchange of value? Am I charging what this is worth, or am I
either undercharging out of insecurity or overcharging
relative to delivery? Be honest.
```

**Note:** *The integrity check question is not rhetorical. The framework is explicit that pricing should reflect a genuine commitment to the customer's flourishing, not a strategy to extract maximum value. Charge what your product is worth, deliver on that price, and the economics take care of themselves.*

# Part Seven: The Art of the Prompt — Getting Expert-Level Outputs

---

# Chapter 20: The Most Effective Way to Prompt AI

---

I've watched plenty of people get seriously mediocre work product out of Claude, ChatGPT, and all the other AI platforms. The pattern is consistent: they ask a vague question, get a vague answer, and then decide AI isn't that useful for real work, and go back to doing things the slow way.

The problem is almost never Claude's capability. The problem is the gap between what they asked for and what they needed to ask for. Prompting is a skill, and like any skill the gap between a beginner and someone who's learned it properly is enormous.

This chapter is about closing that gap. Not just giving you prompts to copy but teaching you the principles that let you write your own prompts for any situation you encounter. The prompts in this book are valuable but the ability to write great prompts from scratch is more valuable because you'll need it for the rest of your business-building career.

## The Principle of Specific Context

The single most impactful change you can make to your prompting: add specific context. Not generic context — specific context.

'Write an email for my health business' is generic context. 'Write a broadcast email for my email list of 3,200 health-conscious women aged 35-50 who subscribed through my gut reset lead magnet. My voice is conversational and honest — I write like I'm talking to a friend who trusts my health knowledge, not like a wellness brand on Instagram. This email is announcing a 3-day flash sale on my fermentation kit bundle. The main objection I need to handle is that people think fermentation is complicated. Subject line should create curiosity.' That's specific context.

Claude doesn't know your business, your voice, your audience, or the specific thing you're trying to accomplish unless you tell it. Everything you don't specify, Claude fills in with defaults. Those defaults are often fine. But 'fine' is not what you're optimizing for.

Before every important prompt, ask yourself: what does Claude need to know to give me something I'd use? Write that down. Add it to the prompt. If you feed Claude actual examples of quality writing you’re proud of from past communications it can do a much better job writing like you do.

## The Five Elements of a Great Business Prompt

The best business prompts contain five elements: Context, Goal, Constraints, Framework, and Evaluation Criteria. They don't always show up in that order, and they don't always carry equal weight. But once you know the five, you start to notice when one's missing — and missing elements are why most prompts come back useless.

Context. The situation Claude is working in. Your business, your customer, your brand, your relevant history. This is the world of the prompt.

A weak version: I run an online business.

A strong version: I run a direct-to-consumer specialty coffee subscription. Three-bag sampler boxes at $49, monthly recurring. Customer base is roughly 60% gift buyers, 40% personal subscribers. Average customer stays subscribed for four months before churning. We pride ourselves on origin storytelling and roaster transparency.

The strong version hands Claude the picture before asking it to do anything. Every output it produces afterward sits inside that picture. The weak version forces Claude to either ask clarifying questions or guess — and guessing is where bad output starts.

Goal. What you want to accomplish. Be explicit.

A weak version: Help me think through pricing.

A strong version: Generate three pricing architecture options for a $297 to $997 B2C digital course targeting busy professionals. Each option should specify the core offer price, the upsell price point, and the rationale behind the spread. Pick price points that match how this audience actually thinks about money.

The strong version is doing three things at once. It tells Claude what to produce (three options, with three components each), what audience to keep in mind (busy professionals), and what range to work inside ($297 to $997). The weak version produces a meandering essay about pricing theory. The strong version produces something you can actually decide on.

Constraints. What limits apply. Voice restrictions. Format requirements. Things to include or avoid. Audience considerations.

Constraints aren't limitations on Claude. They're guidance that focuses the output. The more you can specify, the better the output gets.

Examples of useful constraints:

Write in plain English. No marketing jargon. If you'd say it differently to a friend at dinner, say it that way here.

Don't use the word "leverage" as a verb. Don't use "unlock," "empower," or "transform." Don't open with a rhetorical question.

Output as five separate variations, each labeled. No preamble explaining the variations. No conclusion summarizing them.

This is for SMB owners with no marketing background. Assume they don't know what a CTA or a tripwire is. Define terms or work around them.

Headlines only. No body copy. Each one should stand alone.

A prompt without constraints is a prompt asking for whatever the model thinks you want. A prompt with good constraints is a prompt that produces what you actually need.

Framework. The specific methodology or lens you want applied. This is where strategic sophistication enters the output before Claude writes a single word.

If you tell Claude to write a sales page, you get a sales page. If you tell Claude to write a sales page using PAS — problem, agitation, solution — with the agitation section getting twice the space of the problem section, you get a sales page built on a proven copywriting structure.

Examples of frameworks worth invoking by name:

Apply the Three Levers framework: increase number of customers, increase average transaction value, increase frequency of purchase. Give me five tactical ideas under each lever.

Use the AIDA structure (Attention, Interest, Desire, Action). Each section should be one tight paragraph.

Frame the offer using risk reversal — what does the customer keep if it doesn't work, what do they lose if they don't try.

Treat this as a positioning exercise. Pick a specific corner of the market and defend it, the way Ries and Trout would in Positioning.

If you've read the marketing book that produced the framework, you can name the book and Claude knows exactly what you mean. The model has read the same books you have. Use that.

Evaluation criteria. How you'll judge the output. What makes it successful.

Sometimes this is implicit — if you ask for five headlines under 60 characters each, the criteria are baked into the request. For complex work, state the criteria explicitly. The output gets dramatically better when Claude knows what it's aiming at.

A weak version: Write some email subject lines for me.

A strong version: Write ten email subject lines for a Black Friday promotion. Success looks like: each one is under 50 characters, each one creates curiosity without being clickbait, at least three should not mention Black Friday explicitly, and the whole set should feel like it's from a real person, not a corporate marketing department.

That's not a wishlist. That's a scoring rubric. Claude reads it and writes against it. The output you get back is dramatically closer to usable than a vague request would have produced.

The five elements together

You don't need all five every time. A simple prompt about a simple task can skip Framework and Evaluation Criteria. A prompt for a brand-defining piece of copy needs all five and probably needs them detailed.

The skill isn't memorizing the framework. The skill is noticing, when the output comes back wrong, which element was missing or weak — and fixing that one specifically before running the prompt again.

## The Iteration Protocol

Remember, the first output is a draft, the goal is achieving excellence through a specific feedback and revision process.

Here's the protocol I use for high-stakes work:

Step one: read the output completely before giving any feedback. Don't start editing in your head before you've read the whole thing. Understand what Claude did before you decide what needs to change.

Step two: identify the three to five most specific things that need to change. Not 'make it better' — 'the second paragraph is too formal, the transition at the end of paragraph four doesn't work, the CTA is weak, and the overall tone is correct but the opening hook is generic.' Specific, actionable, prioritized.

Step three: give that specific feedback back to Claude in your next message. It’s important to tell Claude what you liked too, not to be polite but because it helps Claude understand which elements to preserve while fixing the others.

Step four: repeat. Usually two to three rounds of specific feedback gets you to something excellent. If you're still not satisfied after three rounds, the problem might be in the original prompt rather than the execution and you might want to consider rewriting the prompt more specifically.

The common trap is giving up after one round because the output isn't perfect. First drafts are almost never perfect. The second and third drafts, with specific feedback, are usually significantly better.

## Voice Training — Getting Claude to Sound Like You

One of the most valuable investments you can make in your Claude workflow is training it to write in your specific voice. Not perfectly — there will always be an editing pass required — but well enough that the gap between Claude's draft and your published voice is small.

The method: create a voice training prompt that provides real examples of your writing alongside a description of your voice characteristics. The more real writing examples you include, the better Claude's voice approximation becomes.

**✦ VOICE TRAINING PROMPT**

```
I need you to internalize my writing voice so that everything you write for me today sounds like it came from me. Here are examples of my writing — real emails, posts, or copy that I've written: [PASTE 3-5 EXAMPLES OF YOUR ACTUAL WRITING — longer is better, ideally at least 200 words per example] Based on these examples, please describe my voice in terms of:

- Sentence length and structure (do I write long complex sentences or short punchy ones?)

- Formality level and register

- Use of profanity or unconventional language

- Specific phrases or expressions I use repeatedly

- Things I never say (corporate speak, jargon, specific overused phrases)

- How I open emails or pieces

- How I close and sign off

- My use of humor and self-deprecation

- My relationship with the reader — how I talk to them

- The emotional register I typically write in After describing my voice, write a short test piece — a 150-word email about [any simple topic] — in my exact voice. I'll tell you what you got right and what needs adjustment. For all writing tasks in this conversation, default to this voice without needing to be reminded.
```

**Note:** *After Claude describes your voice and writes the test piece, give it specific feedback on what's right and what's off. 'You got the sentence length right but the opening is too formal — I never start with a statement, I usually start with a question or an observation.' That level of specific voice feedback dramatically improves subsequent outputs.*

# Chapter 21: Advanced AI Techniques — Expert Panels, Pre-Mortems, and Devil's Advocates

---

This chapter is for people who have gotten comfortable with basic prompting and want to push further. These techniques produce outputs at a level of strategic sophistication that's impressive — not because Claude is doing magic, but because you're directing it more intelligently.

## The Expert Panel Technique

One of the most powerful advanced prompting techniques is asking Claude to simulate a conversation among several named experts who have different perspectives on your problem.

The experts can be real people — marketing thinkers, business strategists, people Claude knows well from its training. Or they can be archetypes you define — a skeptical CFO, an aggressive growth marketer, a customer-focused product designer. Either way, getting multiple perspectives in the same output surfaces the tensions and trade-offs you'd miss if you only asked one expert at a time. The disagreements between them are usually where the real insight lives.

Here's what that looks like in practice. Say you run a direct-to-consumer skincare brand doing about $80,000 a month, mostly through paid ads on Meta. Customer acquisition cost is climbing, the ad accounts have been throttled twice in the last six months, and you're trying to decide whether to pour more money into ads, build out organic content, launch a referral program, or expand into wholesale and retail. Asking Claude as a generic strategist gets you a generic answer. Convening an expert panel gets you something else entirely.

The prompt might look like this:

"I run a DTC skincare brand at $80K/month, 90% Meta ads, CAC climbing, ad accounts unstable. I'm trying to decide between four growth paths: scaling paid ads, building organic content, launching a referral program, or expanding into wholesale/retail. Convene a panel of four advisors and have them debate this:

— Jay Abraham, focused on hidden assets and underutilized leverage already inside my business — Gary Vaynerchuk, focused on organic content and platform attention — A skeptical CFO who only cares about gross margin, cash flow, and risk — A DTC operator who has run a brand from $1M to $20M and knows what actually scales

Have each one weigh in. Then have them push back on each other where they disagree. End with a synthesis paragraph identifying where they converged and where the real strategic question still sits."

The output you get back isn't a single recommendation. It's a transcript of four perspectives doing real work. Abraham points out that your existing customer list is probably under-monetized — referrals and repeat-purchase sequences likely beat new acquisition spend. Vaynerchuk argues that organic content is the only durable answer to platform risk. The CFO says wholesale margins are too thin to be the answer and the ad spend is the actual problem. The DTC operator says referral programs sound clean on paper but rarely move the needle at this scale, and what really matters is fixing the post-purchase sequence and the email list before doing anything else.

That disagreement is the value. None of those four answers is right alone. The synthesis — what these four would actually agree on if forced to — is usually a clearer strategic direction than any single advisor would have produced.

The trick is picking advisors who genuinely disagree. A panel of four Gary Vaynerchuks gives you one answer, four times. A panel of people who would actually argue with each other gives you the trade-offs you need to see before making a decision.

**✦ EXPERT PANEL STRATEGY PROMPT**

```
I want to run a multi-expert strategic analysis of my
business decision. Here is the decision I'm facing:
[DESCRIBE THE SPECIFIC DECISION – pricing, market entry,
positioning, offer design, growth channel, etc.] Here is the
full context:
```

```
[PASTE YOUR CONTEXT DOCUMENT OR RELEVANT BUSINESS
INFORMATION] Please simulate a roundtable conversation among
these four advisors: 1. JAY ABRAHAM — marketing strategist
who thinks in terms of three levers, preeminence, and
lifetime value maximization

2. A SKEPTICAL CUSTOMER — the most resistant, once-burned
version of my target customer, who will poke holes in
everything

3. AN AGGRESSIVE GROWTH MARKETER — someone who prioritizes
speed and scale, comfortable with risk, focused on customer
acquisition volume

4. A CONSERVATIVE OPERATOR — someone who prioritizes unit
economics, profitability, and sustainable growth over speed
Have them debate the decision, each from their genuine
perspective. Surface the tensions. Let them disagree. At the
end, synthesize: what is the balanced recommendation that
incorporates the valid insights from each perspective?
```

**Note:** *The skeptical customer voice is often the most valuable one. It's easy to convince yourself that an offer is compelling when you're the one who built it. Having Claude simulate the most skeptical version of your buyer challenges your assumptions in a productive way.*

## The Pre-Mortem Technique

A pre-mortem is a strategic exercise where you assume a plan has failed and work backwards to understand why. It's far more useful than a risk assessment because it forces specificity — instead of asking 'what could go wrong?' it asks 'what went wrong?'

**✦ PRE-MORTEM ANALYSIS PROMPT**

```
I'm planning to [DESCRIBE YOUR PLAN — launch, enter a
market, build a funnel, launch a product, etc.] Here are the
full details: [DESCRIBE YOUR PLAN COMPLETELY] Run a pre-
mortem. Assume it's 12 months from now and this plan has
failed badly — not just underperformed, but failed. Revenue
is a fraction of projections. The business is struggling.
From that future vantage point: 1. LIST THE 10 MOST
```

```
PLAUSIBLE REASONS IT FAILED. Not unlikely disasters —
common, realistic ways this type of plan fails. Be specific
about why each failure mode is plausible for MY specific
plan. 2. FOR EACH FAILURE MODE: - What was the early warning
sign that should have triggered a course correction? - At
what point could the failure have been prevented? - What
would I have done differently if I'd anticipated it? 3. RANK
THE FAILURE MODES by: likelihood (how often does this happen
in similar situations?) and impact (how bad would this
specific failure be?). 4. THE TOP 3 RISKS: Focus on the
three highest-priority risks. For each: what specific action
should I take NOW to reduce the probability of this failure?
5. THE RESILIENCE QUESTION: If failures 1 and 2 both happen
simultaneously, is this business still salvageable? What
would recovery look like?
```

**Note:** *The discomfort of the pre-mortem is productive. If a specific failure mode makes you uneasy, that's your nervous system telling you there's a real risk there. Don't dismiss it — address it before you launch.*

### The Devil's Advocate Technique

Before publishing any major piece of copy or launching any offer, run it through a devil's advocate prompt. Ask Claude to read your work as your most skeptical potential customer and tell you exactly what they'd object to.

**✦ DEVIL'S ADVOCATE COPY REVIEW PROMPT**

```
Here is [a sales page / an email / a landing page / an offer
description] I've written: [PASTE YOUR CONTENT] Take the
role of my most skeptical potential customer. This person:

- Has been disappointed by products like mine before

- Reads everything critically and looks for red flags

- Defaults to 'no' unless something convinces them

- Is intelligent and not easily impressed by marketing
language As this skeptical reader, tell me: 1. THE 10 THINGS
THAT WOULD MAKE YOU NOT BUY — specific objections, doubts,
```

```
or red flags this content triggers

2. THE VAGUE CLAIMS — which promises are too generic or
unsubstantiated to be convincing?

3. THE TRUST GAPS — where do you not believe the claims
being made? What would need to happen for you to believe
them?

4. THE MISSING INFORMATION — what questions does this
content leave unanswered that would prevent you from buying?

5. THE ONE CHANGE — if you had to identify the single most
important improvement, what would it be? Be harsh. Be
specific. My goal is to find all the weaknesses before a
real skeptical customer finds them.
```

**Note:** *This prompt is humbling and valuable. It consistently surfaces things you missed because you were too close to the work. Run it on every major piece of copy before you publish. The discomfort is worth it.*

# Part Eight: Go Live — Launch, Learn, and Scale

---

# Chapter 22: Launching — Pre-Launch Preparation and the Six-Day Sequence

---

A launch is two jobs. The first is everything you do before cart opens — technical checks, message checks, contingency plans for what breaks. The second is the email sequence that actually sells during the launch window. Botch the prep and the sequence has nothing to land on. Botch the sequence and the prep was for nothing. This chapter covers both.

## The Pre-Launch Checklist

Launch day is the wrong time to discover that your checkout page doesn't work on mobile. Or that the email automation is firing twice. Or that the upsell link is broken. Or that your payment processor is in test mode.

I know this because I have experienced each of those specific failures at the exact worst moment. They are all fixable. None of them are fixable on launch day without losing sales and sending a professional disaster signal to a segment of your audience.

The pre-launch checklist is not a suggestion. It is a ritual. You run through every element of the system you've built before a single dollar is on the table. Not because you think it'll be broken, but because the cost of finding out it's broken in production is much higher than the cost of the checklist.

## The Technical Checklist

Go through your entire funnel as a customer would. Click every button. Fill out every form with test data. Complete a test purchase using a test payment method. Confirm the right emails fire in the right sequence. Read every email on mobile and desktop. Click every link in every email and confirm it goes where it should.

Specific things to verify: page load speed on both mobile and desktop (use Google PageSpeed Insights — anything below 70 is a problem), mobile responsiveness on every funnel page, form validation errors (do they make sense to a real user?), payment processor mode (absolutely must be live, not test), email delivery to your own inbox (does it land in inbox or spam?), all automation trigger conditions, and every link in every email.

Then give the whole funnel to someone who hasn't seen it. Ask them to go through it as a customer. Watch where they get confused, where they hesitate, what they don't understand. Fresh eyes find things you're blind to after staring at the same pages for weeks.

## The Soft Launch

Before you go to your full list, go to a small segment. Ten percent of your most engaged subscribers, or a specific segment you can target, or a small paid traffic test. Let fifty to one hundred people through the funnel and watch what happens to the numbers.

The specific metrics to watch in the first 48 hours of soft launch: landing page conversion rate, email open rate on the first launch email, checkout completion rate, and order bump take rate. Each of these tells you something specific about whether the system is working.

A landing page conversion rate below fifteen percent on a warm audience is a problem with the page or the offer. An email open rate below twenty percent is a problem with the subject line or a list warmth issue. A checkout completion rate below forty percent is often a friction issue or a pricing trust issue. An order bump take rate below ten percent suggests the bump isn't positioned right.

Fix the problems you find in the soft launch before you open to your full list. This is not slowing down, this is ensuring that when you scale up you're scaling something that works.

**✦ PRE-LAUNCH AUDIT PROMPT**

```
I'm preparing to launch [YOUR OFFER] and I want to do a
thorough pre-launch audit. Here is everything about the
launch: [DESCRIBE YOUR LAUNCH: the offer, the funnel, the
email sequence, the traffic plan, the timeline] Please help
me build a pre-launch audit by: 1. TECHNICAL CHECKLIST: Give
me a complete, specific technical checklist for a FunnelKit-
based launch. Every element that should be tested, in the
order I should test it. 2. COPY REVIEW: I'll paste my main
sales page copy here:

[PASTE YOUR COPY]

Review it for: unsupported claims, unanswered questions,
```

```
weak CTAs, missing social proof, and any place where a
skeptical reader would stop trusting the page. 3. OFFER
REVIEW: I'll paste my offer details here:

[PASTE YOUR OFFER DETAILS]

Is this offer compelling enough? What's the weakest element?
What would most likely cause hesitation at the decision
moment? 4. SOFT LAUNCH PLAN: Design a specific soft launch
protocol. What segment of my list? What metrics should I
track for the first 48 hours? What thresholds define 'go'
vs. 'stop and fix'? 5. CONTINGENCY PLANNING: What are the
three most likely technical failures? What is the specific
response procedure for each? (What do I do, what do I say to
customers who are affected, how quickly can I resolve it?)
6. POST-LAUNCH DEBRIEF SCHEDULE: When and how should I
review results? What's my decision framework for deciding
whether to optimize, scale, or pivot after the launch?
```

**Note:** *The contingency planning section is worth taking seriously. Having a written response plan for 'checkout is broken' or 'email sequence fired twice' means you respond calmly and professionally in the moment rather than panicking. Preparation is the difference between a professional problem resolution and a visible disaster.*

## The Launch Sequence

A great offer is essential, but timing and positioning matter just as much. Even the best offer will fail if you present it to cold prospects, frame it poorly, or launch it at the wrong moment. When you get the positioning right — warm audience, clear framing, strategic timing — the same offer converts at rates that transform your business economics.

This section is about the strategic decisions around offer positioning: when to make the ask, what context creates the highest purchase intent, how to frame the transition from value to sale, and how to handle the moments when people get close but don't buy.

## The Buyer Journey and Purchase Intent

Purchase intent varies enormously across the customer journey. Someone who just heard about you for the first time is at the lowest possible purchase intent — they don't know you, haven't experienced your value, and have no particular reason to trust your promises. Someone who has been on your list for three months, has read fifty of your emails, gotten genuine value from your lead magnet, and has been waiting for you to offer exactly this product is at the highest possible purchase intent.

Matching your offer presentation to where the customer is in that journey is one of the most important variables in conversion optimization.

The mistake many businesses make is presenting the full offer to cold audiences and wondering why conversion rates are low. Cold audiences need education and trust-building before they're ready to buy. Presenting the offer before that groundwork is done is like asking someone to marry you on a first date — it's technically possible, but with a very low success rate.

Warm audiences — people who have consumed your content, received your emails, experienced your free value, they're ready for the offer. Making them wait too long after they're ready, or being timid about presenting the offer when they've pre-qualified themselves, is the opposite mistake.

## The Soft Offer Vs. The Hard Offer

There are two fundamental ways to present an offer, soft and direct.

A soft offer introduces the product in the context of related value: 'This is the principle I teach in [product]. If you want to go deeper, here's the link.' No pressure, no urgency, no CTA emphasis. It's almost an aside.

A hard offer is the direct sales pitch: 'Here's exactly what's included, here's exactly what it costs, here's exactly what you get, and here's the link to get it. This offer is available until [deadline].'

Both have their place. Soft offers are right for early in the relationship — when you're still building trust and want to mention that something exists without making it feel like every email is a pitch. Hard offers are right for launch sequences, when someone has shown strong buying signals, and when the warm-up work has been done.

The ratio most email businesses aim for: three to five soft mentions or warm-up emails for every hard offer email. The trust is built through the consistent delivery of value; the revenue is generated through the periodic, clear, well-timed hard offers.

**✦ OFFER LAUNCH SEQUENCE PROMPT**

```
I'm planning a launch for my offer. Here's the context:
OFFER: [Full description and price]

AUDIENCE: [Who is on the list — how warm are they? How long
```

have they been subscribed? What's the existing relationship?]

LAUNCH WINDOW: [How many days is the cart open?]

URGENCY MECHANISM: [What's the real reason to buy now – deadline, price change, bonus expiration, limited quantity?]

BRAND VOICE: [Your voice] Design a complete launch email sequence: 1. PRE-LAUNCH PHASE (3-5 days before cart opens): 2-3 emails that warm up the audience, hint at what's coming, and build anticipation WITHOUT revealing the offer yet. These should create curiosity and desire without a hard pitch. 2. CART OPEN SEQUENCE (the launch period – typically 5-7 days): - Day 1: Launch announcement email. This is the reveal – what it is, why now, full offer details. - Day 2: Value email. No pitch. Just deliver something useful related to the offer topic. Builds trust and serves people who aren't ready yet. - Day 3-4: Social proof email. Results, testimonials, case studies that prove the promise. - Day 5: Objection handler. Address the 3 most common reasons someone hasn't bought yet. Be empathetic and specific. - Day 6: Urgency reminder. The deadline is approaching. Remind them without being pushy. - Day 7: Final call. Cart closes today. This is your most direct email – final chance, clear CTA, specific urgency. 3. FOR EACH EMAIL: Write the complete email (subject line, preview text, full body, CTA, P.S.) 4. POST-LAUNCH EMAIL: One email for buyers (celebrating the decision, setting expectations for what happens next) and one email for non-buyers (acknowledging the cart is closed, not shaming, keeping the relationship warm, hinting at next steps). Apply the Strategy of Preeminence: every email should feel like it's from someone invested in the reader's success, even the sales emails.

**Note:** *The post-close emails are ones most businesses skip. The email to buyers that celebrates their decision and sets clear expectations dramatically reduces buyer's remorse and refund rates. The email to non-buyers that keeps the relationship warm is how you protect the list for your next launch.*

# Chapter 23: How to Read Your Data Like a $500/Hour Marketing Consultant

---

Data is only useful if it tells you something actionable — not just 'we made X dollars' or 'conversion rate was Y percent,' but 'this specific thing underperformed in this specific way, which suggests this specific change would improve results.' That level of diagnostic reading is the skill that separates businesses that consistently improve from businesses that run the same campaigns and get the same results.

## The Diagnostic Framework

Every funnel has a critical path — the sequence of steps a prospect takes from first encounter to first purchase. Each step in that path has a conversion rate, and that conversion rate is a diagnostic signal.

Email open rate is the first diagnostic. Low open rates on launch emails are almost always a subject line problem or a list warmth problem. Subject line problems are fixable immediately by testing new subject lines. List warmth problems require either more time building the relationship or a different segmentation strategy.

Landing page conversion rate is the second diagnostic. Low landing page conversion suggests either a mismatch between the traffic source and the page content, an offer that isn't compelling enough for the audience, or a page experience issue (design, load time, mobile performance). Each has a different fix.

Checkout conversion rate is the third. High abandonment at checkout is most commonly a trust issue (not enough social proof near the payment form), a friction issue (too many required fields, confusing flow), or a price shock issue (the price landed wrong in context). Test each hypothesis sequentially.

Watch how many buyers add the bump and accept the upsell. That number is your scoreboard for both offers. If it's low, the offer's wrong, the price is wrong, or the way you're presenting it is wrong. Three things to check, in that order.

**✦ LAUNCH DATA ANALYSIS PROMPT**

```
My launch just completed. Here is all the data: EMAIL
SEQUENCE PERFORMANCE:

- Send 1 (subject: [X]): open rate [X%], click rate [X%]

- Send 2: open rate [X%], click rate [X%]

- [Continue for all launch emails] FUNNEL PERFORMANCE:

- Total visitors to landing page: [N]

- Opt-ins or product page views: [N] ([X%] conversion)

- Checkout page views: [N]

- Completed purchases: [N] ([X%] checkout conversion)

- Order bump take rate: [X%]

- Upsell take rate: [X%] REVENUE:

- Gross revenue: [$X]

- Number of orders: [N]
```

```
- Average order value: [$X]

- Refunds/chargebacks: [N] QUALITATIVE:

- Customer feedback received: [paste any emails, comments,
messages]

- Customer service issues that came up: [describe] Please
analyze this data and tell me: 1. WHAT WORKED: Which
elements performed above what you'd expect for this type of
launch? What should I preserve exactly? 2. WHAT
UNDERPERFORMED: Where are the clearest gaps between expected
and actual performance? What is the most likely diagnosis
for each? 3. THE ONE HIGHEST-LEVERAGE FIX: If I could only
change one thing before my next launch, what would it be and
why? 4. TEST HYPOTHESES: Identify 3 specific A/B tests I
should run in my next launch. For each: what's being tested,
what's the hypothesis, what result would confirm or
disconfirm it? 5. BUSINESS IMPLICATIONS: What does this data
suggest about my market, my audience, my offer, or my
positioning that should inform my strategy beyond just this
launch? Be direct. Tell me what the numbers say, including
things I might not want to hear.
```

**Note:** *The 'things you might not want to hear' instruction is important and underused. Without it, Claude tends toward diplomatic framing that softens the message. For diagnostic work, you want the unfiltered analysis.*

# Chapter 24: The A/B Testing Discipline That Replaces Guesswork With Knowledge

---

For forty years before the internet existed, direct response companies ran split tests. You'd mail list A with one offer and list B with a slightly different one. You'd run two different TV spots in two different markets. You'd print the magazine ad with one headline on the east coast and a different one on the west coast, and then you'd count which one produced more calls. Later we would run separate 800 numbers for each creative.

We invented split testing because we had to. There was no other way to know if you were right. Opinion doesn't move product, the phone rings or it doesn't.

That discipline is what separates the people who build real businesses from the ones who argue about button colors in Slack all day. A/B testing is not a trick. It is the mechanism by which you replace guessing with knowing, one variable at a time, until your funnel actually does the thing it was built to do.

There are three mistakes most operators make when they split test, and almost everyone makes the same three. Know what they are and you're already ahead of ninety percent of the people running tests on their funnels right now.

## The Three Mistakes That Waste Your Tests

**Testing things that don't move the needle.** The single most common failure mode in online A/B testing is the button color test. Somebody read a blog post from 2009 where changing a button from green to red lifted conversions by twenty-three percent on some page somewhere, and now they're spending a week split-testing button colors on their checkout page. It's the junk food of optimization. Even if you win, the lift is small and the attention you spent on it is attention you didn't spend on the headline, the offer, or the guarantee — which is where the real money is.

The rule I use: test things that, if they win by a real margin, would change how I think about my business. A headline test that wins by twenty percent teaches me something about what my customer cares about. A button color test that wins by two percent teaches me nothing I can act on.

**Testing too many things at once.** If you change the headline AND the hero image AND the bullets AND the CTA at the same time, and the page converts better, you don't know which change did the work. You have a win you can't replicate and can't build on. One variable per test. One change at a time. It's slower, but the knowledge compounds.

**Calling a winner before you have one.** This is the biggest one. Somebody runs a test for three days with ninety-four visitors on variant A and a hundred and eleven on variant B. Variant B got four conversions. Variant A got two. They declare B the winner and roll it out.

What they actually have is random noise. Two-versus-four on samples that small tells you nothing. Run the same test again and the result could easily flip.

Sample size is boring and it matters enormously. As a rough rule: three hundred conversions per variant before you trust a result, and more than that for smaller lifts. For most small business funnels that means a test runs for weeks, not days. That's fine. The test keeps running in the background while you build the next thing.

## What To Test, In Priority Order

If all your tests should be things that could move the needle, here is the order that actually does.

**Headlines first.** Your headline is the single highest-leverage element on any page. It determines whether the reader stays or leaves, and almost everything else on the page is arguing for the promise the headline made. One winning headline test is worth twenty button-color tests.

**Offers second.** The structure of the offer — what's included, how it's priced, what the guarantee is, what the payment structure looks like — produces bigger conversion swings than any copy change can. Three payments of thirty-seven versus one payment of ninety-seven is worth testing. Thirty-day guarantee versus sixty-day guarantee is worth testing. These are offer-structure tests, and they change how you handle what you're actually selling, not just how you describe it.

**Pricing third.** Rarely tested because people are nervous about it. Pricing is one of the cleanest things to test in a funnel. Try the higher number. You will be wrong about what your market will pay more often than you think, and almost always in the direction of undercharging.

**Risk reversal fourth.** The guarantee, the return policy, the trial length, the cancellation terms. Every element that reduces the buyer's perceived risk is test-worthy. A stronger guarantee often produces a bigger conversion lift than anything you can do with copy.

**CTA language fifth.** "Start My Free Trial" versus "Get Instant Access" versus "Reserve My Spot." Worth testing once the big things are locked in. The lift is usually modest, but it's directionally useful and cheap to run.

**Button color last, if at all.** Almost never the highest-leverage use of your time.

## The Cadence

You should always have at least one serious A/B test running on the highest-leverage page in your funnel, at all times. That's the baseline. When it concludes — meaning it reaches significance or you give up and call it inconclusive — you document what happened, roll the winner into production, and start the next one.

Document everything. A simple log: date started, hypothesis, variant A, variant B, sample size, result, what you learned. Over a year you will have twenty or thirty tests documented. That record is one of the most valuable assets your business has. It tells you what your customer actually responds to, not what you think they respond to, and those are usually different things.

Here is the compounding math. You don't need home runs, a twenty percent lift on your headline, a fifteen percent lift on your offer, a ten percent lift on your checkout process — each one modest — compounds to more than a fifty percent improvement in funnel economics. That's the game. Not one miracle test but a disciplined cadence of small, rigorous tests stacked over time.

## When Not To Test

A test is a luxury that requires traffic. If your funnel is getting two hundred visitors a month, you don't have enough volume to run a meaningful A/B test on it. Fix that first. Get the traffic, then test.

In the meantime, the substitute for statistical testing is qualitative research. Talk to customers. Read the emails they send you. Watch session recordings if your analytics supports it. Read the forum threads where your market hangs out and note the exact language they use. One good customer interview will teach you more than any underpowered test on two hundred visitors.

### How FunnelKit Runs The Test For You

One of the practical arguments for FunnelKit Pro as the funnel engine is that A/B testing is built into it. You don't need a separate optimization platform, you don't need to set up Google Optimize (which Google shut down anyway), and you don't need to wire up a third-party split-testing tool that may or may not play nicely with WooCommerce. The testing engine lives inside the funnel builder itself.

Here's how it works in practice. You open any funnel — opt-in page, sales page, checkout page, order bump, one-click upsell, or thank you page — and you add a variant. FunnelKit gives you a choice: duplicate the existing version and modify it, or build a new variant from scratch. For most tests, duplicate the control and change only the one element you're testing. The rule is one variable at a time, and duplicating keeps everything else identical by default.

Once your variant exists, you set the traffic distribution. Fifty-fifty is the standard split. FunnelKit also lets you weight it unevenly — seventy-thirty, ninety-ten — which is occasionally useful when you're testing a risky new variant against a proven control and you want to limit the downside. For most tests, stick with fifty-fifty and let the numbers do the work.

As soon as you click Start the traffic begins splitting between the two variants. FunnelKit's analytics section tracks conversions on each until you've accumulated enough data to have a clear winner. The winning variant now gets one hundred percent of the traffic, the losing variant is archived, and you start the next test.

Tech Tip: if you have a caching plugin running on your WordPress site you need to exclude your funnel pages from the cache while a test is running. Cached pages don't serve the variant logic correctly and you'll end up with skewed data that quietly invalidates the test. This is a five-minute fix in any caching plugin's settings but it's the kind of thing that can kill a test without you realizing it.

For email testing FunnelKit Automations has its own split-testing layer. Broadcast emails support variant testing — you write a control email, add a Variant A with a different subject line or different body copy, and FunnelKit sends each to a portion of your list and tracks which performs better. The Smart Sending option is particularly useful here: you define a sample size, FunnelKit sends to that sample, waits for results, and then automatically sends the winning variant to the rest of your list. It's the same principle as a direct mail A/B split, automated for scale.

The automation side also supports split-path testing. If you want to test a three-email sequence against a two-email sequence, or a ten-percent-off coupon against a fifteen-percent-off coupon, you can branch the automation and let the numbers tell you which path produces more downstream revenue. This is a more sophisticated test and usually worth running only once you have significant list size, but it's there when you're ready for it.

The point of all this is that the tool is built to handle the mechanics. All you have to do is design tests worth running, document what you learn, and make the next test smarter than the last. FunnelKit handles the splitting, the tracking, and the analytics.

## Where Claude Fits

Claude is excellent at generating test variants. You tell it what the page is, what the hypothesis is, who the customer is, and ask for ten headline alternatives worth testing. You read them, pick the two strongest challengers, and run the test. When the test concludes, Claude helps you think through what the result means and what the next test should be. The bottleneck in most testing programs — coming up with good variants to test — stops being a bottleneck.

What Claude doesn't do is replace the discipline. You still have to run the tests. You still have to wait for significance. You still have to document what you learned. The tool accelerates the thinking around the test. The test itself is yours to run.

**✦ A/B TEST DESIGN PROMPT**

```
I'm designing an A/B test for my funnel. Here's the context:
THE PAGE AND ELEMENT: [Which page, which specific element –
headline, offer structure, price, guarantee, CTA, etc.]
CURRENT CONTROL: [Exact current version – paste the
headline, offer, or copy as it appears now] CURRENT
PERFORMANCE: [Current conversion rate and approximate
traffic volume on this element] MY CUSTOMER AVATAR: [Core
pain, identity, desired outcome] MY HYPOTHESIS: [What do I
believe would make this convert better, and why?]
Please help me design a rigorous A/B test:
1. CHALLENGER VARIANTS: Generate five possible challenger
variants to test against the control. For each: the exact
version, the strategic theory behind it (why would this
outperform?), and what result would confirm or disconfirm
the theory.
2. RECOMMENDED CHALLENGER: Of the five, which is the
strongest candidate and why? What does it uniquely test that
the others don't?
3. SAMPLE SIZE ESTIMATE: Given my traffic volume,
approximately how long would this test need to run to
produce a trustworthy result? What's the minimum number of
conversions per variant I should aim for before calling a
winner?
4. THE DIAGNOSTIC: If the challenger wins, what does that
tell me about my audience? If it loses, what does that tell
me? Make sure the test teaches me something either way.
5. THE NEXT TEST: Assuming this test completes, what's the
natural follow-up test that builds on what I learn from it?
What's the logical testing sequence over the next three
tests?
```

**Note:** *The diagnostic question is the most important one in this prompt. A test that doesn't teach you anything about your customer regardless of which variant wins is a test not worth running. Design tests where both outcomes produce actionable knowledge — that's what separates a testing program from random tinkering.*

# Chapter 25: Scaling — How to Grow What's Working Without Scaling What's Broken

Once you have a funnel that converts, an offer that lands, and an email sequence that builds real relationships the game changes. Now you’re ready to scale.

Scaling is not doing more of everything. That's how you scale your problems as well as your successes. Scaling is deliberately increasing the things that are working while eliminating or fixing the things that aren't.

## The Scaling Sequence

Here's the sequence I follow when something is working and I want to grow it.

First, understand it. Before you scale, understand why it's working. Not just that conversion rates are good but what specifically is driving that. Is it the headline? The offer structure? The guarantee? The specific audience segment you were targeting? The traffic source? Scale something without understanding it and you risk accidentally breaking the thing that's making it work.

Second, stabilize it. Can you run this funnel ten times in a row and get consistent results? Or does performance vary dramatically between launches? Variability is the enemy of confident scaling. If results are inconsistent, find the source of variability and address it before you pour money into traffic.

Third, optimize everything. Before scaling volume, optimize value per customer. Add or improve the upsell. Test a higher-priced offer. Improve the email sequence that drives repeat purchase. Getting the per-customer economics right at small scale is much easier than trying to fix them under the pressure of large-scale operations.

Fourth, add traffic. Once the economics are solid and the system is stable, scale the traffic. Use paid ads if the economics support it. More content. Better SEO. More partnerships. The mechanism depends on your market and your strengths. Don't invest in traffic until the destination is optimized to convert it.

### The Content Compound

One of the highest-leverage activities for sustainable long-term growth is building a content library that compounds over time. Every piece of useful content you publish is an asset that continues attracting attention and building trust for years.

Content marketing doesn't pay off fast — this is why so many businesses abandon it. A blog post you write today might generate minimal traffic for six months. By month twelve, it's generating meaningful search traffic. By month twenty-four, it's one of your primary organic lead sources.

Claude makes content creation faster than it has ever been. It’s not instantaneous, the content still requires your expertise, your perspective, and your editing to be good rather than generic. But the draft creation, the structure design, the research synthesis, the SEO optimization — all of this goes faster with Claude. The goal is to create a sustainable content calendar that you can maintain, not a burst of thirty pieces in January that stops by March.

**✦ 90-DAY GROWTH PLAN PROMPT**

```
My launch has completed and the business has momentum. Here is where I stand: CURRENT STATE: [Revenue, list size, conversion rates, what's working, what isn't]

GOALS FOR NEXT 90 DAYS: [Specific, measurable goals]

CONSTRAINTS: [Budget, time, team size, technical limitations] Build me a specific 90-day growth plan that applies the three-lever framework: LEVER ONE — CUSTOMER ACQUISITION:

- What is the highest-leverage addition to my customer acquisition system right now?

- What specific channel should I invest in next? What does the test plan look like?

- What content should I be creating to build organic traffic? LEVER TWO — TRANSACTION VALUE:

- Is there an upsell or order bump I should add or optimize?

- Is there a higher-priced offer I should develop?

- Is there a bundle opportunity that increases average order value? LEVER THREE — PURCHASE FREQUENCY:

- What email or retention improvements would increase how often existing customers buy?

- Is there a subscription or continuity model that makes sense?

- What community-building activity would increase engagement and loyalty? THE PLAN:

- Month 1 priorities (3-5 specific, measurable actions)

- Month 2 priorities (contingent on Month 1 results)

- Month 3 priorities (contingent on Month 2 results)
```

```
- Weekly metrics I should track

- Decision rules: when to accelerate, when to stop and
reassess Be specific. Generic growth plans are useless.
```

**Note:** *The contingent planning structure — Month 2 depends on Month 1 results — is intentional. Plans that don't adapt to new information become obsolete immediately. Build in decision points from the start.*

# Reference Section: Operations, Traffic, and Growth

The chapters in this section address operational topics that become relevant as your business develops. Use them when the topic is current for you, not necessarily in order.

## Getting Traffic — The Honest Guide to Filling Your Funnel

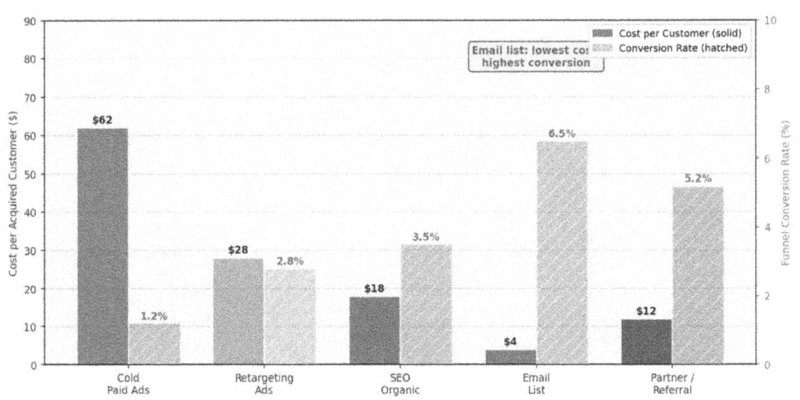


You can have the best funnel in the world, the most irresistible offer, and copy that would make a professional copywriter weep with envy. None of it matters if nobody sees it.

Traffic is the fuel that makes the funnel machine run. Without it, everything else is theoretical. With it, the system you've built starts producing.

For most businesses the hard truth that nobody wants to tell you is that there is no easy traffic source. Every channel requires something from you — money, time, skill, patience, or some combination of these. Anyone promising effortless viral growth or instant paid traffic that converts at magical rates is probably trying to sell you a course.

What there is are traffic channels that are well-suited to different businesses at different stages, with different trade-offs between cost, speed, volume, and quality. Understanding those trade-offs is what lets you choose the right channels for where you are and where you're going.

## The Traffic Trade-Off Framework

Every traffic channel involves trade-offs across four dimensions: cost, speed, quality, and scalability.

Cost is self-explanatory — how much money does it take to acquire each visitor, lead, and customer? Paid advertising has explicit, measurable cost. Content marketing has lower direct cost but significant time cost. Referrals have low cost but limited scalability without a deliberate program. SEO has low ongoing cost but requires significant upfront investment.

Speed is how quickly the channel generates results. Paid advertising can send traffic immediately. SEO takes months to years before significant organic traffic appears. Referrals work on their own timeline. Content compounding is slow at the start and accelerates over time.

Quality is the conversion rate and lifetime value of the customers acquired through each channel. Referrals typically produce the highest-quality customers, people recommended by someone they trust. Organic search produces high intent customers who found you while actively looking for what you sell. Cold paid traffic produces the widest variance, it can be excellent or terrible depending on targeting and creative.

Scalability is the ceiling on how much traffic the channel can produce. Referrals are low-ceiling in the absence of a formal program, content marketing is medium-ceiling, and paid advertising is theoretically unlimited as long as the economics support the spend.

No channel is best on all four dimensions. The right channel depends on your stage, your resources, and your goals.

## Organic Traffic — Content, Community, and SEO

Organic traffic is traffic that doesn't require ongoing payment per visitor. It comes from search engines, from social media posts, from community participation, from referrals. The defining characteristic is that once the asset is created — a well-ranked blog post, a popular YouTube video, an active community presence — it continues generating traffic without continued investment.

The trade-off is time. Building organic traffic is slow. A new blog requires months to years before search engines trust it enough to rank it meaningfully. A YouTube channel requires consistent output before the algorithm starts surfacing it. But the compound effect of organic traffic is real and significant: the traffic that flows from a well-ranked piece of content five years after it was created is pure margin, requiring no ongoing spend.

For businesses at the early stage, I recommend a specific organic strategy: find the communities where your target customer congregates and become a useful member. Don't do this as a promotional exercise but as a real participant who provides value. Answer questions, share relevant knowledge, engage authentically. Over time, this builds the reputation and relationships that drive organic traffic to your funnel. It also gives you continuous, free access to the language, questions, and problems of your market.

Content marketing builds on this community presence. The best content answers the specific questions your target customer is already asking, in the communities they're already in, in language they use. Use Claude to help you identify those questions and structure content that answers them thoroughly.

### Paid Advertising — Speed at a Cost

Paid advertising is the trade of money for traffic. It's the fastest path to volume, but it requires the unit economics to support it — and the unit economics require a well-built funnel.

This is why paid advertising comes after funnel optimization in the business building sequence. You never want to discover that your offer doesn't convert by paying for traffic. Validate the offer with warm audiences first — your own list, partnerships, organic social. Then, once you've confirmed it converts, add paid traffic to scale what's already working.

The major paid channels each have different characteristics. Meta ads (Facebook and Instagram) are excellent for audience targeting based on demographics, interests, and behaviors. They work particularly well for consumer products and personal transformation offers where emotion and visual storytelling drive purchase intent. The cost has risen significantly over the years but the targeting sophistication remains unmatched.

Google Search ads target people who are actively searching for what you sell. The traffic quality is often exceptional because the person is already in a buying mindset — they searched for a solution to a specific problem. The cost can be high in competitive markets, but conversion rates are typically higher than cold social traffic.

YouTube ads fall between the two — visual like Meta, intent-based like Google, excellent for businesses where education and demonstration matter to the purchase decision.

I'm not going into the mechanics of paid advertising in this book because that's a deep enough topic to deserve its own volume — and because the fundamentals change faster than most printed books can keep up with. What I can give you is the strategic framework for knowing when you're ready for paid traffic and how to approach it.

**✦ TRAFFIC STRATEGY PROMPT**

```
I need to develop a traffic strategy for my business. Here
is my full context: BUSINESS: [What you sell, who to, at
what price]

FUNNEL: [Describe the funnel you're driving traffic to –
lead magnet, free plus shipping, direct offer, etc.]

CURRENT TRAFFIC: [What traffic do you have now? Zero? Some
organic? A small list?]

BUDGET: [Monthly budget available for traffic testing – be
honest]

SKILLS: [Are you comfortable with paid ads? Content
creation? Video? Community building?]

TIMEFRAME: [When do you need meaningful traffic – urgently
or can you play the long game?] Please design a traffic
strategy: 1. CHANNEL PRIORITIZATION: Given my situation,
which traffic channels should I focus on first, second, and
```

```
third? For each recommended channel: why it's right for my stage and situation, what the realistic ramp-up looks like, what I need to have in place before starting. 2. ORGANIC FOUNDATION: What organic traffic activities should I be doing regardless of paid budget? Which communities, what content format, what participation strategy? 3. PAID TRAFFIC READINESS ASSESSMENT: Am I ready for paid traffic? What metrics would tell me my funnel is ready to have money poured into it? What would cause paid traffic to be premature? 4. FIRST 90-DAY TRAFFIC PLAN: Specifically, what traffic activities should I do in the next 90 days to get to [TARGET NUMBER] of qualified visitors to my funnel? 5. TRAFFIC ECONOMICS: At my current funnel conversion rates (or estimated rates), what does my maximum viable cost-per-click look like? What does that tell me about which paid channels are economically viable?
```

**Note:** *The readiness assessment is the most important section if you're eager to run ads. The most common expensive mistake in online business is turning on paid traffic before the funnel is tested and the offer is proven. Do not skip this step.*

## Strategic Partnerships as a Traffic Source

I want to return to partnerships as a traffic mechanism because they are consistently underutilized and can be extraordinarily effective at a stage when paid advertising is not yet economical.

Partnership marketing works by finding win-win relationships: you help a business serve their customers better, and they introduce you to those customers. For example, if you sell time management courses, partner with productivity software companies. You provide valuable training to their users; they provide you access to people who already care about productivity. Both parties win, and the customer gets genuinely useful resources.

The key insight that makes partnerships work is that you're not asking someone to give you their audience for free. You're bringing them something of value — often a percentage of revenue, sometimes a co-branded offer, sometimes a reciprocal promotion to your own audience. The partnership works because both parties benefit, and the deal is structured to make that obvious.

A single well-executed partnership with a business that has ten to twenty thousand relevant subscribers can outperform months of paid advertising at a fraction of the cost — the traffic quality tends to be excellent because the partner's recommendation carries their credibility.

Use Claude to identify partnership candidates, assess the potential fit, and draft the outreach email. The creativity in partnership development is in the structure of the deal — finding the arrangement that makes both parties eager to say yes. Claude is good at helping you think through the options.

# Analytics — What to Measure and How to Act on It

Business data tells stories, but most people don't know how to read them. They log into their analytics dashboard, see a wall of numbers, feel vaguely informed, close the tab, and keep doing what they were doing. This is not the same as being data-driven. Being data-driven means having specific numbers you track for specific reasons, reviewing them on a specific cadence, and having decision rules that tell you what to do when those numbers are above or below specific thresholds.

That level of rigor sounds complicated but it isn't. For most businesses at the stage this book is aimed at, the metrics that matter fit on a single page. The sophistication comes not from tracking more things but from tracking the right things and responding to what they tell you.

## The Metrics That Matter

Let me give you the metrics hierarchy. These are the numbers that tell you whether your business is healthy and growing, organized from most to least important.

Revenue. Total revenue, split by source (funnel, direct, email-driven). This is the outcome metric — the thing all other metrics are in service of. Review weekly.

Customer acquisition cost (CAC). What does it cost to acquire one new customer? Divide your total marketing and advertising spend by the number of new customers acquired in the same period. This number tells you whether your acquisition economics are sustainable. If your CAC is higher than your first-purchase revenue, you're losing money on every customer and relying entirely on repeat purchase to recover — which requires an excellent retention system and a long time horizon.

Average order value (AOV). What does the average customer spend per transaction? This is your lever-two metric — it tells you how well your upsell and order bump system is working. Low AOV when you have upsells in place usually means the upsells are poorly positioned or priced.

Email engagement. Open rates, click rates, and reply rates. These are the health metrics of your most important customer communication channel. Declining open rates signal either list fatigue (emailing too frequently), content relevance issues (sending things people don't care about), or deliverability problems (your emails are going to spam).

Repeat purchase rate. What percentage of customers buy more than once within twelve months? This is your lever-three metric. A business with a high repeat purchase rate has fundamental advantages in unit economics — it can afford to spend more to acquire customers because it knows they'll keep buying.

List growth rate. How many new subscribers are joining your list each week, and what's the net growth after unsubscribes? A shrinking or stagnant list is a long-term threat to the business. A consistently growing list is an asset that compounds.

### Setting Up Your Dashboard

Your metrics dashboard doesn't need to be elaborate. It needs to be something you look at consistently.

I use a simple document — literally a Google Sheet — that I update every Monday morning. It has a row for each week and columns for the six metrics I described above plus two or three business-specific ones I've added over time. Each cell is either green (at or above target), yellow (within acceptable range but trending wrong), or red (below threshold, requiring attention).

The simple color-coding is not decorative. It creates a visual pattern that tells the story of the week in ten seconds. Three red cells on a Monday morning is not a fun experience, but it's the kind of information that triggers productive action rather than comfortable ignorance.

For the underlying data: Google Analytics 4 handles web traffic and funnel behavior. Your email platform handles email metrics. WooCommerce reports handle revenue, AOV, and repeat purchase data. FunnelKit's built-in analytics handles funnel conversion rates. You don't need a sophisticated Business Intelligence tool at this stage. You need to pull the relevant numbers from these sources into your weekly review.

**✦ METRICS DASHBOARD DESIGN PROMPT**

```
I want to set up a simple, actionable metrics dashboard for my business. Here is my business context: BUSINESS MODEL: [What you sell, how, the main funnel types]

STAGE: [Early, growing, established?]

CURRENT TRACKING: [What are you currently tracking, if anything?]

MAIN GOALS: [What are you trying to achieve in the next 12 months?] Please design my metrics dashboard: 1. THE CORE METRICS: What are the 6-8 numbers I should track every week? For each: define it precisely, explain what it measures, describe what a healthy range looks like for my business type, and describe what action to take when it's outside that range. 2. THE REVIEW CADENCE: What should I review weekly vs. monthly vs. quarterly? Some things change too slowly to review weekly; some change too fast to review only monthly. 3. THE EARLY WARNING INDICATORS: What are the leading indicators – numbers that tell me something is about to go wrong before the revenue impact shows up? (e.g., declining email open rates are a leading indicator of declining email revenue) 4. DECISION RULES: For my 3 most important metrics, write a simple decision rule: 'If [metric] drops below [threshold] for [time period], I will [specific action].' 5. THE VANITY METRIC AUDIT: What metrics might I be tempted to track that would make me feel good without telling me anything useful? (Social media follower counts, total page views without conversion context, etc.) Warn me away from them.
```

**Note:** *The decision rules are the most important part. Analytics without decision rules produces informed inaction — you know what's happening but you don't have a clear trigger for doing something about it. Write the rules. Commit to following them.*

## Using Claude to Interpret Your Data

Claude is useful for data interpretation — especially for identifying non-obvious patterns in your business metrics. You can paste your weekly numbers directly into a Claude session and ask for an interpretation.

The key to useful Claude data analysis is providing context, not just numbers. 'My email open rate dropped from 28% to 19% this week' is a number. 'My email open rate dropped from 28% to 19% this week. This week I sent three emails instead of the usual one, and the subject lines were more promotional than usual. My list grew by about 300 people this month through a new partnership, and those people have only been on the list for 2-3 weeks.' That context lets Claude give you a diagnostic interpretation rather than generic observations.

Use this approach for any metric that surprises you — either pleasantly or negatively. When something works better than expected, understanding why is just as important as when something underperforms. The good surprises are your clues to what to do more of.

# Customer Experience and Retention — The Overlooked Edge

---

This chapter is about something that most marketing books don't spend enough time on, what happens after someone buys.

The vast majority of online business content is about acquisition — getting new customers. There's a reason for this: acquisition is visible, measurable, and exciting. New customer numbers are a clear metric of growth. Traffic, conversions, revenue from new sales — all of it is quantifiable and satisfying.

What's less visible is the customer relationship after purchase, and this is where the majority of a business's long-term value gets built or destroyed. The customer who had a great buying experience and received even greater post-purchase care is the customer who buys again, who refers friends, who defends your brand in community discussions, who becomes loyal in a way that makes your business model incrementally better over time.

The customer who had an adequate buying experience and then heard nothing, or who had a problem and found your customer service slow and dismissive — that customer is not a customer anymore. And in the era of social proof and community-driven purchasing decisions, the actively dissatisfied customer is an ongoing liability.

### The Economics of Retention

Research across industries consistently finds that selling to an existing customer costs five to seven times less than acquiring a new one. Existing customers convert at two to three times the rate of cold prospects. They spend more per transaction, they trust you more, they don't need to be persuaded from scratch, and they refer new customers (which are the highest-quality leads you can acquire).

A business with a repeat purchase rate of thirty percent is fundamentally more valuable and more efficient to run than a business with a repeat purchase rate of ten percent, even if their customer acquisition numbers are identical. The thirty-percent-retention business generates three times the revenue from its customer base and can afford to invest more in acquisition because the lifetime value math supports it.

Retention is built through the accumulation of small things done right. The post-purchase email that arrives within an hour with practical information about the product. The follow-up email three days later checking whether they have questions. The thirty-day email checking in on their experience. The moment when they have a problem and it's resolved quickly and generously, or the surprise upgrade or bonus that arrives unexpectedly. Each of these moments is a small investment in a relationship that compounds.

## The Post-Purchase Experience Design

Design your post-purchase experience the way you'd design a first date: you want the other person to leave excited, confident they made the right decision, and looking forward to seeing you again.

The confirmation email should arrive immediately and should be warm and human, not just a receipt. Tell them exactly what happens next. If it's a physical product, when will it ship and how will they track it? If it's a digital product, where do they access it and what should they do first? If it's a service, what does onboarding look like and who will they hear from?

Eliminate the anxiety of the post-purchase moment. Every person who clicks buy feels a small version of buyer's remorse in the minutes after — a question of whether they made the right call. Your job is to immediately and specifically answer that question in the affirmative. They made the right call. Here's why. Here's what happens next.

The day-three follow-up email is about engagement — making sure they've started using what they bought and offering proactive help. Don’t wait for them to have a problem and reach out, check in and ask. This proactive follow-up is rare enough in most businesses that it stands out dramatically when you do it.

Use Claude to design and write this entire post-purchase sequence. Give it the product, the customer, the brand voice, and the specific concerns a new buyer might have and ask it to write a sequence that makes every new customer feel well taken care of.

**✦ POST-PURCHASE EXPERIENCE DESIGN PROMPT**

```
I want to design a complete post-purchase experience for my customers. Here is everything relevant: PRODUCT: [What they bought – physical, digital, service?]

DELIVERY: [How and when do they receive it? What's the delivery experience?]

COMMON NEW CUSTOMER CONCERNS: [What questions or anxieties do new buyers typically have?]

MY CAPACITY: [What can I realistically do for each customer – automated vs. personal touches?]

BRAND VOICE: [How you communicate] Please design a complete post-purchase sequence: 1. IMMEDIATE CONFIRMATION EMAIL (fires within 2 minutes of purchase): Purpose is to eliminate buyer's remorse, confirm the right decision, and set clear expectations. Write this email completely. 2. DAY 3 FOLLOW-UP: Check in, make sure they've received/started/engaged with the product, offer proactive help. Write this email completely. 3. DAY 10 EXPERIENCE CHECK-IN: Check on their experience, gather qualitative feedback, invite any questions. Write this email completely. 4. DAY 30 MILESTONE EMAIL: Celebrate something – their decision, any progress they might have made, the value they've gotten. Soft mention of next product or upgrade. Write this email completely. 5. CUSTOMER SERVICE PROTOCOL: How should customer problems be handled? Write the response template for the 3 most common customer service issues in my product category. 6. THE WOW MOMENT: What is one unexpected, delightful thing I could do for new customers that would make them tell someone about it? It should cost less than $15 per customer in either time or money.
```

**Note:** *The 'wow moment' is not about spending a lot of money. It's about exceeding expectations in a specific, personal way. A handwritten note. An unexpected bonus that arrived with the* *product. A personal email from you specifically referencing something they mentioned. These small gestures create disproportionate loyalty.*

## Handling Problems with Grace

Problems happen. Products get damaged in shipping. Digital downloads don't work on certain devices. Customers misunderstood what they were buying. Instructions weren't clear enough. These situations are inevitable, and how you handle them is one of the most powerful relationship-building opportunities you have.

The standard poor response to a customer problem: slow acknowledgment, defensiveness about whose fault it is, a solution that feels grudging, and a sense that the customer got what they were owed and nothing more. This response turns a problem into a permanent negative impression.

The excellent response to a customer problem is fast acknowledgment (within a few hours if possible), immediate ownership regardless of fault, a generous solution that clearly communicates 'your satisfaction matters more to me than this cost,' and a follow-up to confirm the resolution was satisfactory.

The surprising truth about customer problems is that if handled graciously a problem can increase loyalty beyond what it would have been if the problem hadn't occurred. This is called the service recovery paradox, and it's real. A customer who had a problem and had it resolved generously is often more loyal than a customer who never had a problem, because they've seen your values in action under pressure.

Use Claude to draft your customer service response templates, these are the responses to the most common problems you encounter. The templates save time and ensure that every customer gets the same excellent response regardless of who handles the issue or what time it is.

# Building Authority — Why Experts Get the Customers

---

There is a question underneath almost every buying decision that never gets asked out loud: Why should I trust you?

A customer looking at your offer is simultaneously processing a visible layer — what you're selling, what it costs, what it does — and an invisible one. The invisible layer is the credibility assessment. Who is this person? Do they know what they're talking about? Have other people trusted them and been glad they did? What gives them the right to be the one I learn this from?

Building authority, meaning establishing genuine credibility in your market is not a vanity project, it’s the foundation that makes your marketing work. This chapter is about how to build it deliberately, quickly, and honestly.

## What Authority Actually Is

Authority is not the same as fame. It's not the same as credentials. It's not about having a PhD or having been on television or having a hundred thousand Instagram followers.

Authority means your target audience believes you know what you're talking about. You just need to consistently share useful knowledge with the right people.

The most powerful form of authority for a direct-to-consumer business is lived experience authority: you have done the thing, you have the results (or have helped others get them), and you speak from experience rather than theory. This is why the brand story matters so much — it establishes the foundation of your authority by showing that you've been where your customer is and found a way through.

Right behind it is demonstrated knowledge — you prove, again and again, that you know your space cold. No ego, just the consistent quality of what you put out. A market researcher who shows their process earns authority. A copywriter who breaks down their frameworks earns authority. A nutritionist who explains the reasoning behind their recommendations earns authority. The knowledge has to show up consistently, in public, where people can see it.

### The Content Authority Loop

Content is the fastest legitimate route to authority at any stage of business development. The mechanism is simple and reliable: publish useful, specific, accurate content in your area of expertise, in the places your target audience spends time, consistently over time. The accumulation of that content creates an authority impression which hard to fake and hard to compete away.

The critical word in that description is specific. Generic content doesn't build authority. 'Ten tips to be healthier' belongs to nobody. 'Why every fermentation troubleshooting guide gets the temperature question wrong, and what the research says' belongs to whoever published it. Specificity is what creates the authority impression.

The content authority loop works like this: you publish a specific, useful piece of content. A portion of the people who encounter it find it valuable and remember who provided it. Some of them share it. Some of them seek out your other content. Some of them follow you or join your list. Your credibility with that growing audience builds as they consume more of your content. When you eventually make an offer, they buy from an authority they trust rather than a stranger they're evaluating.

Claude helps you produce content at a volume and quality level that would be nearly impossible to sustain manually. It doesn't replace the expertise — you have to know what's worth saying. But it dramatically accelerates the process of getting what you know into publishable form.

## Borrowed Authority and Social Proof

Authority is also transferred. When someone whose authority you already respect endorses you, their credibility flows to you. This is why podcast interviews, collaborations with established creators in your niche, guest posts on respected publications, and testimonials from recognized people in your market are so valuable at the early stages before you've built your own authority footprint.

Borrowed authority is not cheating. It's legitimate, durable credibility — as long as the endorsement is genuine. A recommendation from someone who has used and benefited from your product carries real authority. A paid sponsorship from someone who has never used your product is different and audiences can increasingly feel the difference.

In the early stages of building your business, actively seek opportunities for borrowed authority. Reach out to podcast hosts in your niche for interviews, offer to guest write for publications your audience reads, and ask satisfied early customers for testimonials that you can use prominently. These early credibility signals accelerate the authority-building curve significantly.

Claude helps you identify the right opportunities and craft the right outreach. The pitch for a podcast interview, the proposal for a guest post, the testimonial request — all of these have structures and angles that work, and Claude can help you find them for your specific situation.

**✦ AUTHORITY BUILDING PLAN PROMPT**

```
I want to build genuine authority in [YOUR MARKET] for my business [DESCRIBE IT]. Here is my current status: CURRENT AUTHORITY LEVEL: [None yet / Some recognition in community / Established but not widely known]

MY GENUINE EXPERTISE: [What do you know? What have you done? What results do you have?]

MY AUDIENCE: [Where do they congregate? What do they read? Who do they listen to?]

MY CONTENT CAPACITY: [How much time per week can I spend creating content? What format am I comfortable with — writing, video, audio, social posts?] Please design a 6-month authority building plan: 1. AUTHORITY AUDIT: Based on my stated expertise and current status, what authority do I legitimately have right now? What's my honest starting point? 2. AUTHORITY GAPS: What would my target audience most want to see from an authority in my space that I currently can't demonstrate? How do I close those gaps? 3. CONTENT STRATEGY: What content format is best for building authority in my specific market? What topics should I own? Give me a 6-month content calendar concept — themes by month, not individual pieces. 4. BORROWED AUTHORITY TARGETS: Identify 10 specific podcasts, publications, or creators in my market I should pursue for collaboration. For the top 3: what angle would make them interested in having me? 5. PROOF ARCHITECTURE: What specific evidence should I be systematically collecting — case studies, testimonials, results, credentials — to build visible proof of my authority over the next 6 months? 6. THE MILESTONE: What would 'established authority' look like for me in this market, specifically? What would be different about my business and my standing in the community?
```

**Note:** *The audit question is uncomfortable and important. Most people overestimate their perceived authority relative to what the market sees. Starting from an honest assessment of your current standing rather than your desired standing leads to a more effective plan.*

## A Note on Authenticity

I want to say something about authenticity because it's a word that gets used a lot and means almost nothing when used vaguely.

In the context of building authority, authenticity means that you only claim the expertise that you have. Don't present results you didn't achieve or pretend your journey was smoother than it was. Don't adopt a persona that isn't yours.

The practical reason this matters, beyond ethics, is that authenticity is much easier to sustain long-term. A manufactured persona requires constant maintenance, it creates a gap between what you project publicly and who you are, and that gap is exhausting to manage and eventually creates inconsistency that audiences can feel.

Your genuine story — including the failures, the confusions, the wrong turns — is more compelling than a polished narrative of unbroken success. The market has seen polished narratives. They're everywhere. What's rare and connecting is someone who says: “here's what I did, here's what went wrong, here's what I learned from it, here's what worked”. That honesty is a form of authority in itself.

# Questions People Ask — And Honest Answers

---

After years of talking publicly about this approach to building online businesses, I've heard a lot of the same questions. Here are the ones that come up most often, with the most honest answers I can give.

### Does any of this still work if the market is crowded?

Yes, with an important qualification: a crowded market requires more specific positioning, not a different approach. The tools and frameworks in this book work specifically well in crowded markets because they force the kind of differentiation that most businesses in crowded markets aren't doing.

Most businesses in crowded markets compete on generic terms — better quality, lower price, more features. The positioning work in Part Three and the customer avatar work in Part Two are specifically designed to find the underserved sub-segment within a crowded market where you can win without competing on generic terms.

The fermentation market is crowded. The gut health market is crowded. The digital marketing education market is astronomically crowded. But within each of those crowded markets, there are specific customer segments with specific pains that none of the crowded-market players are specifically serving. Those gaps exist in almost every market. Finding them is a matter of looking carefully rather than hoping for an uncrowded space.

### Can Claude write in my voice, or will everything sound AI-generated?

Claude can get close to your voice with proper setup and iteration, but 'close' is not the same as 'indistinguishable.' The outputs will always need editing. The question is not whether they'll be perfect on the first pass — they won't be — but whether the editing gap is small enough that the workflow is worthwhile.

In my experience, for most people, it is. Getting a draft that's eighty percent right and editing it to one hundred percent takes less time than writing from scratch, especially for tasks that require structural thinking as well as writing.

The way to close the gap: invest in voice training as described in Chapter Twenty-Two. Provide Claude with real examples of your writing before you ask it to write in your voice. Give specific feedback on what it gets right and wrong in the first several sessions. The model gets better at your voice over the course of an extended session — the more context it has about what you sound like, the closer the outputs get.

And be honest with yourself about what 'your voice' is. Most people have a looser, more variable voice than they realize. The things that truly define your voice — specific phrases you use, your relationship to profanity, your degree of self-deprecation, your opening and closing habits — those can be described and trained. What's harder to train are the idiosyncratic references, the specific memories and experiences that only you have, and the genuine feeling of a specific human sensibility. Those elements always require your hand on the work.

**How do I know if my offer is priced right?**

You price it and test it. There is no purely analytical answer to this question — pricing is ultimately validated by market response, not by calculation.

That said, the analytical work I described in Chapter Twenty gives you a range to test within. Value-based pricing gives you a ceiling — what the transformation is worth to the customer. Competitive analysis gives you the existing market reference points. The floor is the price below which you're working for free.

Within that range, test. Launch at a specific price, measure conversion rate, measure refund rate (too-high refund rates are often a sign of pricing misalignment), and get qualitative feedback from both buyers and non-buyers about price. The signal from non-buyers is often more useful than the signal from buyers — 'I didn't buy because the price felt high for what I understood the value to be' is actionable information.

The specific thing most people are afraid to test: pricing higher. The instinct is to price low to maximize volume, but in many markets and at many price points, higher pricing increases both conversion rate and customer quality. The customers who self-select at a higher price point are often more committed, get better results, and generate fewer support issues. Test higher before you assume you need to go lower.

### I don't have an audience yet. Where do I start?

You start by building the list, and you build the list by being useful to the community where your target customers already are.

This is the advice nobody wants because it doesn't sound like a hack or a shortcut. But it's the honest answer and it's durable — find the places where your target customer spends time, forums, subreddits, Facebook groups, Discord servers, whatever is relevant to your market. Participate genuinely, answer questions, share knowledge. Do this for six to twelve months with consistency.

During this same period, build the lead magnet funnel. Have something to offer when people ask for more from you. The community participation drives traffic to the lead magnet, the lead magnet builds the list, and the list becomes the foundation for everything else.

There are faster paths, paid advertising can build a list quickly, but they require a tested offer and a working funnel before they make economic sense. Organic community building is slower but produces higher-quality subscribers and builds authority simultaneously. Do both, give it eighteen months, and the compounding becomes the unfair advantage you didn't have when you started.

### How long before I see real revenue?

If you define 'real revenue' as 'enough to quit a day job,' twelve to twenty-four months is a reasonable expectation for someone doing this seriously and correctly. Some businesses generate meaningful revenue in six months; others take three years. The variance is enormous and depends on market selection, offer quality, list size, consistency of effort, and frankly, luck.

If you define 'real revenue' as 'any revenue that demonstrates the model is working,' most people following this process can get to their first customer within ninety days of starting seriously. That first customer proves the concept. The path from first customer to sustainable revenue is mostly about volume and optimization — doing more of what's working.

Set a realistic timeline for yourself and put milestones in it. By month one: lead magnet live, funnel built. By month three: list at 500 subscribers, first offer tested. By month six: list at 1,500, first $5,000 in revenue. By month twelve: list at 5,000, $2,000-3,000 monthly recurring. These are not guarantees — they're benchmarks that tell you whether you're on a trajectory worth continuing.

### Is Claude going to replace my need for a team?

For most businesses in the early and growth stages this book is aimed at — absolutely not, and that's the honest answer. Claude replaces some of the work that used to require specific specialist hires, particularly in copy, market research, and strategic consultation. It does not replace the need for human judgment, human relationships, or human creativity at the strategic level. But when you're starting out, especially under financial constraints, there's nothing wrong with being a team of one, in fact, sometimes it's better that way.

As businesses scale, the team needs that emerge are usually in operations, customer service, and specialized execution that benefits from human judgment and accountability. Claude doesn't make those needs disappear — it delays them by helping solo and small-team operators maintain a higher output level with fewer people.

The healthy way to think about it is that Claude is an amplifier. It makes you more effective at your existing skills and extends your capacity into adjacent skills you don't fully have. It doesn't make you omnipotent. You still need human collaborators, advisors, and eventually staff. You just need them later and for different things than you would have without AI tools.

### What if I follow all this and it still doesn't work?

Then you learn something real, and you adjust.

I want to be direct about this because I think a lot of business education implicitly promises that doing the right things guarantees success, and that's simply not true. You can do everything in this book correctly and still choose a market that turns out to be too small, or underestimate the distribution difficulty, or run into timing bad luck, or simply not be the right person for that particular opportunity.

Failure is not evidence that you did something wrong. Sometimes it's just information. What did you learn about the market? What did you learn about your own strengths and weaknesses? What would you do differently in the next attempt?

The best entrepreneurs I've observed treat failure as expensive data rather than as evidence of their own inadequacy. They build, they learn, they adjust, they rebuild. The tools and frameworks in this book are yours to keep regardless of how any specific venture goes. The market research skills, the offer design skills, the prompting skills, and the copy skills transfer. Even a failed business attempt builds the toolkit.

The only permanent failure is stopping entirely. Everything else is a learning loop. Like so many other things described in this book, multiple intelligent iterations are often the key to success.

# A Week in the AI-Augmented Business — What This Looks Like

---

Books about systems and frameworks can sometimes leave you with a clear understanding of the principles and a fuzzy sense of what using those principles looks like day to day. So let me give you a concrete, specific account of what a working week using the framework in this book looks like.

What follows is a composite week — not a single real week, because real weeks are messy and non-linear — but a representative picture of how the tools, principles, and workflows interact in an ongoing business. I've shaped it around a hypothetical business: someone selling a premium home bread baking course with a strong community component and an email list of about four thousand people. The specifics are not important; the rhythm and the decisions are.

## Monday: Review and Strategy

Monday mornings start with the metrics review. Fifteen to twenty minutes with the weekly dashboard — revenue, email engagement, funnel conversions, list growth, repeat purchase rates. This week, open rates are down slightly on Thursday's email but click rates held. Checkout conversion on the funnel is about where it's been. List grew by 47 new subscribers, above the weekly average.

The email open rate dip is worth investigating. A Claude session: paste the subject line from Thursday's email, the list segment it went to, the content summary, and any unusual context for the week. Ask for the three most likely explanations for the open rate dip and what data would confirm each hypothesis. Claude comes back with the observation that the subject line was more promotional than usual and the email was sent on Thursday when the list typically has lower engagement than Tuesday or Wednesday. Both are worth testing — but neither requires immediate panic.

The list growth number is pleasing. Last week a small partnership produced a batch of new subscribers through a co-promotion. These subscribers are tagged as coming from the partnership, which means they'll get a slightly different welcome sequence that acknowledges how they found the list. This is easy to set up in FunnelKit, a single tag triggers a different welcome automation; it means these subscribers feel immediately recognized rather than landing in a generic sequence.

Ten minutes of strategic thinking: what are the priorities this week? A new product idea came up in the community last week, an advanced technique module that existing students have been asking for. Now is not the time to build it, but it's worth spending fifteen minutes with Claude scoping the idea before it gets forgotten. A quick prompt: here's the request I'm hearing from my community, here's what they already have, here's the gap they're describing — what would the outline of an advanced module look like, and what would be the natural price point? Save the output to the idea file, and revisit next planning cycle.

### Tuesday: Content and Email

Tuesday is the main content day. Today's deliverables are the weekly email to the list and a piece of content for the community forum that can repurpose as a social post.

The email this week is about troubleshooting overproofed dough — a question that came up multiple times in the community forum and in DMs. This is Claude's wheelhouse: a specific technical topic the business owner knows deeply, where Claude helps with structure, opening, and flow.

Paste in the context document. Then the prompt: 'Write a weekly email for my bread baking list about diagnosing and recovering from overproofed dough. The hook should be based around the community question I mentioned — someone posted a photo of a collapsed loaf and said it was their fourth in a row. Open with that energy, the frustration, the mystery, the feeling that you're doing everything right and still failing. Then teach the actual diagnosis, how to tell the difference between underproofed and overproofed, the poke test, what the dough should feel and look like at different stages. Give them something actionable they can do differently this weekend. Close with the connection to the broader skill, that reading the dough is a tactile thing that develops over time, not just from reading instructions.' Voice: a baker talking to another baker. Warm. Real.

First draft comes back solid. The hook is close but slightly too dramatic — tone it down to match the list's expectation. The middle section on the poke test is excellent; keep it almost verbatim. The close is generic — push it further into the specific emotional arc of the learning process. Give that feedback explicitly. Second draft — publishable with minor edits. Total time in Claude session about twenty-five minutes, editing and publishing another fifteen — for a total of forty minutes for a high-quality weekly email.

The community post repurposes the core diagnostic section — a single focused tip with a clear image description request for a visual. Claude reformats the relevant section from the email into a forum-appropriate post, about 150 words, that takes about five minutes.

### Wednesday: Funnel Work

Wednesday is reserved for funnel and product work. Today's project is a new opt-in sequence for people who enter the funnel through a different lead magnet than the primary one — an 'essential bread tools' checklist that's been driving high-quality opt-ins from a YouTube channel partnership but isn't integrated with the existing welcome sequence in a specific enough way.

The session starts with reviewing the existing welcome sequence, reading every email to understand the arc. The new subscribers coming from the tools checklist are a slightly different entry point than the primary lead magnet audience — they're showing interest in the setup and gear side of bread baking but not necessarily the technique side that the main sequence leads with.

Claude session: provide the context, the existing welcome sequence for reference and the specific lead magnet these subscribers used. Write the first three emails of an alternate welcome sequence that acknowledges their specific entry point and transitions them toward the technique content that's the core of the course. These emails should: confirm the right choice in Email 1 by speaking specifically to the tools orientation, deliver value in Email 2 from the perspective of someone who's assembled the right tools but wants to make sure they're using them effectively, and bridge in Email 3 to the bigger skill question — the tools only work as well as the technique behind them — which sets up the primary course.

This kind of specific sequence customization would have been a significant project before AI assistance — thinking through the logic, writing three emails from scratch, getting them right. Today it takes about ninety minutes total including the strategic thinking before the session. The output quality is good enough that the emails need editing but not restructuring and they publish within the week.

## Thursday: Research and Opportunity Scan

Thursday is the planning day for thinking and researching.

The community forum and the main bread baking subreddits get a thirty-minute read. Not casual scrolling but deliberate attention to what questions are coming up repeatedly, what frustrations are persistent and what successes are people celebrating. A running document captures verbatim language. This is the ongoing market research that feeds everything downstream.

This week three separate threads in two different forums mention the same problem: people are making beautiful loaves at sea level but can't figure out why the same recipe fails at altitude. This is a specific, recurring, unsolved pain point. The market research document gets updated. A quick Claude session "what are the actual mechanisms that cause high-altitude bread baking to behave differently? What are the specific adjustments needed, and what's the specific logic behind each one"? Claude produces a solid technical summary. This goes into the idea file for a potential lead magnet, a potential course module, or a potential content series.

The second Thursday task — a competitive landscape scan. Once per month spend thirty to forty-five minutes reviewing what the main competitors in the market are doing. What new products have they launched? What are people saying about them in the forums? What are they apparently not addressing? This scan takes less time than it used to because Claude can help synthesize review patterns quickly by pasting in a batch of recent reviews from a competitor's product and ask for the most common themes in the negative ones.

Thursday ends with updating the weekly plan document: what worked this week, what didn't, what research produced, what's moving to next week's priorities.

### Friday: Customer Service and Community

Friday is for the people who are already in the ecosystem — customer emails, community engagement, any outstanding issues.

Most customer service can be handled quickly with templates — but the templates need to feel personal, not template-like. Claude helps draft templates that read as genuine and warm while covering the predictable situations: the student whose download link isn't working, the customer who wants to know if the course is right for them before they buy, the student who completed the course and wants to know what's next, the person requesting a refund.

Each template gets a specific note reminding whoever is sending it to personalize the first sentence with something from the customer's actual email. This small step transforms a template into a personal response.

Community engagement is not delegated to Claude. This is human time — reading what people are posting, responding genuinely, celebrating their wins, offering help when they're struggling. No AI can replicate the relationship-building value of consistent, genuine human presence in a community. This is where the authority gets built, the loyalty gets cemented, and the early signal of what the market needs comes from.

The week ends with a quick Friday afternoon debrief: What did we publish? What are the metrics compared to last Friday? What's the priority for next Monday? Fifteen minutes of documentation that makes Monday morning's review better.

## What This Adds Up To

What I've described above is approximately twelve to fifteen hours of deliberate, focused work across the week. Not twelve to fifteen hours of being available and reactive — twelve to fifteen hours of building and improving the business. The rest of a normal work week might be spent on the operational side: fulfillment, supplier relationships, administrative tasks, or other work if this is still a side business.

Without AI tools, the same outputs — one email, one community post, one new email sequence, a market research synthesis, competitive review — would take significantly longer. The email alone would be one to two hours instead of forty minutes. The new sequence would be most of a day rather than ninety minutes. The research synthesis would require a lot of manual pattern recognition rather than a twenty-minute Claude session.

The time savings compound over months. Those hours redirect into deeper thinking, better strategic decisions, more customer engagement, more content — the compounding work that builds a business into something durable.

That is the real value proposition of this entire approach. Not just better outputs — reclaimed time that goes back into the high-leverage activities that AI can't do for you.

# Closing: The Long Game

---

I want to end this book the way I'd want any book in this genre to end: honestly.

Building a real business — not a side hustle, not a temporary income stream, but a genuine business that replaces a salary and gives you real freedom — takes two to four years of consistent, intelligent effort. Sometimes less, often more. It requires showing up when results are slow. It requires iterating on failures without taking them personally. It requires building the kind of genuine expertise and genuine customer relationships that can't be faked or cut short.

The tools in this book make that process faster and less expensive than it has ever been. Claude compresses research and strategy work that used to take weeks into hours. FunnelKit Pro lets you build marketing infrastructure that used to require a development team. The leverage is real and the advantage it provides is real.

Leverage amplifies what you bring. If you bring genuine curiosity about your market, genuine commitment to your customer's outcomes, and genuine willingness to keep improving, then this leverage is extraordinary. If you bring half-hearted effort and hope that the AI does the heavy lifting — the leverage amplifies that too, and you get mediocre results faster.

## The Preeminent Business

The Strategy of Preeminence is not just a marketing framework. It's a philosophy of how to run a business that deserves to succeed.

A preeminent business is invested in its customers' outcomes. It communicates honestly rather than manipulatively. It designs offers that deliver real value rather than appearing to deliver value. It handles problems with grace. It earns loyalty through consistent excellence rather than clever retention tricks.

When you build a business this way — with genuine care for the people you serve, genuine commitment to delivering what you promise, and genuine investment in getting better at what you do — it becomes nearly impossible to compete away. You build something that isn't just a funnel or a list or a set of products. You build a relationship between a specific voice and a specific community. The funnel is the infrastructure. That relationship is the real asset.

## What Comes Next

**◆ You now have the blueprint for a One-Person Marketing Department. The tools are real. The system works. The only variable is how seriously you execute it.**

Here's the order of operations from here.

If you haven't done the market research: start there. The research is the foundation, and rushing past it costs you later.

If you've done the research but haven't built your list: lead magnet funnel, first. Build the list before you worry about the product.

If you have a list but haven't made an offer: design the offer and send the launch sequence. Your list is an asset and it depreciates if you don't use it.

If you've launched and have customers: optimize the funnel, build the email sequences, work on repeat purchase. The first customers are your most valuable feedback.

At every stage: prompt the AI, review the outputs, apply your judgment, edit to your voice, publish. Repeat.

This is the process. There is no single launch that makes everything work. There is only the patient, intelligent accumulation of improvements over time. The businesses built by people who treat this as a craft rather than a lottery ticket are the ones still running in five years.

After forty years of watching direct response businesses succeed and fail, I can tell you that the ones that built something lasting all had one thing in common: they kept going when it got hard, and they kept getting smarter about what they were doing. The tools have changed, but the discipline hasn't.

Go build something real. Use the tools. Ask better questions. Take care of your customers.

Then come tell me about it.

— Brian

# Glossary

---

These are the marketing terms I use throughout the book. Plain English definitions, alphabetical order. If a word snagged you while you were reading, here's what it means.

## A

**A/B Test** — Showing two versions of the same thing to different visitors and measuring which one performs better. Also called a split test. The only reliable way to know what actually works versus what you think works.

**AIDA** — Attention, Interest, Desire, Action. Hundred-year-old direct response framework for structuring sales copy. Still works because it mirrors how human buying decisions actually unfold.

**Anchoring** — Showing a high price first so the price you actually want to charge feels like a bargain by comparison. The $497 tier next to the $97 tier makes the $97 tier feel like a gift.

**AOV (Average Order Value)** — What the average customer spends per transaction. Order bumps and upsells are the levers that move this number.

**Authority** — When your audience believes you actually know what you're talking about. Built through consistent, useful content over time. Different from credentials. Different from fame.

**Avatar** — One specific person you're writing for. Not a demographic. Not "millennials." A real person with a real problem, in language they actually use. Sometimes called the customer avatar.

## B

**Borrowed Authority** — When somebody more established vouches for you and their credibility transfers. Podcast interviews, guest posts, testimonials from known names. The fast lane while you build your own authority.

**Bounce Rate** — In email: the percentage of messages that didn't deliver. In web analytics: the percentage of visitors who landed on a page and left without doing anything.

**Broadcast Email** — A one-off email written and sent when you have something specific to say. Different from drip emails that fire automatically on a schedule.

## C

**CAC (Customer Acquisition Cost)** — What it costs you to land one new customer. Total marketing and ad spend divided by new customers in the same period. If your CAC is higher than what a customer is worth to you, you're losing money on every sale.

**Call to Action (CTA)** — The specific thing you're asking the reader to do. "Buy now." "Reply to this email." "Click here to register." Without one, the reader does nothing.

**Cart Abandonment** — Somebody added something to their cart and didn't check out. Often recoverable with a follow-up email sequence. A surprising amount of revenue hides in this category.

**Challenge Funnel** — A short structured experience (usually five days) that ends with an offer. Converts well because by day five the participant has done real work and has results to show for it.

**Charm Pricing** — Prices ending in 7, 9, or 99. ($97 instead of $100.) Helps for discount positioning. Hurts for premium positioning. Don't use it on your high-end offers.

**Cold Traffic** — People who don't know you. Found you through an ad or a search and have no relationship yet. Hardest to convert.

**Content Marketing** — Publishing useful, specific content consistently in places your audience already is. Slow to pay off. Compounds for years if you stick with it.

**Conversion Rate** — What percentage of visitors take the action you wanted. Buy. Opt in. Click. The most diagnostic number you'll track.

**Copy** — Words written to sell something. Different from regular writing because it has a job to do.

**CPC (Cost Per Click)** — What you pay each time somebody clicks your ad.

**CPM (Cost Per Mille)** — What you pay per thousand impressions of your ad. Mille is Latin for thousand.

**Customer Avatar** — See Avatar.

## D

**Devil's Advocate Prompt** — Asking the AI (or a real human) to attack your work and find every weakness. Run it before you publish anything important. Saves you from finding the holes after launch.

**Direct Response** — Marketing built to make somebody act now. Not branding. Not awareness. The phone rings or it doesn't.

**Downsell** — A reduced version of your offer presented after somebody declined the main upsell. Recovers some revenue from people who said no the first time.

**Drip Campaign** — A series of emails that fire on a schedule after somebody joins your list. Builds the relationship in the background while you focus on other things. Also called a drip sequence.

**DTC (Direct-to-Consumer)** — Selling straight to the buyer instead of through retail or distribution. You keep more of the margin and you own the customer relationship.

## E

**Engagement** — How actively your subscribers respond to you. Open rates, click rates, replies. The difference between a dead list and a live one.

**Expert Panel Prompt** — Asking the AI to simulate a conversation between several specific experts about your problem. Surfaces tradeoffs you'd miss asking just one.

## F

**Free-Plus-Shipping Funnel** — Offering a physical product for free, charging only for shipping. Acquires real buyers (with payment information on file) at near-zero net cost.

**Funnel** — The sequence of steps a stranger goes through to become a paying customer. Called a funnel because volume narrows at each step.

**Funnel Builder** — Software that lets you build sales funnels without code. FunnelKit Pro is the one this book recommends.

**Funnel Conversion Rate** — The percentage of people who entered the funnel and made it all the way to the sale. The most useful health metric for the system.

## G

**Guarantee** — What you promise the buyer if the product doesn't deliver. Stronger guarantees produce higher conversion AND lower refund rates. Counterintuitive but consistently true.

## H

**Hard Offer** — A direct pitch. Here's the product, here's the price, here's the link. No subtlety. The right move during launches and once warm-up work is done.

**Headline** — The first words on a page or in an email. The most important words you'll write. The headline either earns the next sentence or you've lost the reader.

**Hero** — The voice and identity behind the brand. The person your subscribers feel they know. Not a logo, a personality.

**Hook** — The opening that earns attention in the first three seconds. A question, a story, a surprising claim. Without it, nothing that follows gets read.

## L

**Lead Magnet** — Something valuable you give away free in exchange for an email address. Checklist, guide, template, mini-course. Builds the list.

**Lead Magnet Funnel** — The full sequence: lead magnet offer to opt-in page to confirmation to welcome sequence to first product offer. Most common starting funnel for new businesses.

**List** — The collected email addresses of people who opted in to hear from you. Owned by you, not by Meta or Google. The most useful asset most online businesses have.

**Long-Form Sales Page** — A sales page that goes long because the buyer needs every objection answered before they're ready. Short-form leaves objections unanswered. Answered objections convert.

**LTV (Lifetime Value)** — Total money one customer generates for your business over the entire relationship. Determines how much you can afford to spend acquiring them. Sometimes written CLV (Customer Lifetime Value).

## M

**Margin** — What's left after costs. Gross margin equals revenue minus cost of goods. Net margin equals revenue minus all costs. Knowing both keeps you honest about what's actually working.

**Market Selection** — Choosing which group of customers to serve. The single highest-leverage decision in the business. Pick the wrong market and nothing downstream saves you.

**MRR (Monthly Recurring Revenue)** — Predictable revenue from subscriptions or memberships you can count on every month. Compounds by design. A small MRR base changes how a business feels.

## N

**Niche** — The specific corner of a market where you can win. "Health-conscious women over 50 who've tried five diets" beats "people interested in health." Pick narrow on purpose.

**Nurture** — The slow-burn relationship-building emails between launches. Not selling, not asking for anything. Just consistent presence.

## O

**One-Click Upsell** — An offer that fires after the first purchase, accepted with a single click. No re-entering payment information. Dramatically more profitable than asking for a second purchase from scratch.

**Open Rate** — What percentage of subscribers opened a given email. Below 20 percent is usually a subject line problem. Below 15 percent is usually a list health problem.

**Order Bump** — A small additional offer presented as a checkbox on the checkout page. Customer adds it without re-entering payment info. Twenty to thirty percent take rates are normal. Adds five to fifteen percent to revenue from work you already did.

## P

**PAS (Problem, Agitation, Solution)** — Classic copywriting structure. Identify the problem, deepen the pain, present the solution. Reliable framework for sales copy.

**Positioning** — Who you serve, what you do for them, why you're the right choice. The three sentences your business should be able to answer in your sleep.

**Post-Purchase Sequence** — The emails that fire after somebody buys. Confirms the decision, sets expectations, sets up repeat purchase. Most businesses skip this entirely. Big mistake.

**Pre-Mortem** — Pretending the project has already failed and asking why. Forces specificity in a way regular risk assessment doesn't.

**Preeminence** — Jay Abraham's framework. Position yourself as the trusted advisor whose first concern is the customer's outcome, not the sale. Sells more in the long run than acting like a vendor.

**Preview Text** — The snippet of email content that shows in the inbox preview next to the subject line. Free real estate most senders waste.

**Prompt** — The instruction you give an AI. Quality of the prompt determines quality of the output. The skill this book is partly about teaching.

**P.S.** — The line at the end of an email after the sign-off. Gets read almost as often as the subject line. Don't waste it.

## R

**Retention** — Keeping customers after the first sale. The difference between a business and a treadmill.

**Risk Reversal** — Putting all the risk of the purchase on yourself instead of the buyer. Strong guarantees, refund policies, performance promises. The stronger the reversal, the higher the conversion.

**ROI (Return on Investment)** — What you got back divided by what you spent. The number that decides whether a channel keeps getting budget.

## S

**Sales Page** — A dedicated page whose only job is to convert. Long-form usually outperforms short-form for considered purchases.

**Sample Size** — How many people went through a test before you can trust the result. Two-versus-four sales is not a test. Three hundred conversions per variant is a real test.

**Segmentation** — Sending different messages to different groups on your list based on what you know about them. Higher relevance, higher conversion, less list fatigue.

**SEO (Search Engine Optimization)** — The work of making search engines surface your content. Slow to pay off. Compounds for years if you do it right.

**Service Recovery Paradox** — A customer whose problem you solved well becomes more loyal than a customer who never had a problem. Counterintuitive but consistently true.

**SMB (Small and Medium Business)** — The target customer for most of what this book describes. One owner, sometimes a small team, no marketing department.

**Social Proof** — Evidence from other customers that your thing works. Testimonials, case studies, results. Necessary because nobody trusts the seller's claims alone.

**Soft Offer** — Mentioning your product in passing inside a value email. "This is the principle I teach in [product]." Almost an aside. Builds awareness without feeling like a pitch.

**Split Test** — See A/B Test.

**Strategy of Preeminence** — See Preeminence.

**Subject Line** — The words that decide whether your email gets opened. Worth more attention than most senders give them.

## T

**Tag** — A label attached to a subscriber in your email platform that records what they've done, what they're interested in, where they are in your process. Without tags, you broadcast to everyone the same way. With tags, you talk to people based on their actual behavior.

**Three Levers** — Jay Abraham's growth framework. Get more customers, increase what they spend per transaction, get them to buy more often. Every growth move pulls one of these three. Most businesses ignore the second and third.

**Tripwire** — A low-priced first offer (usually $7 to $37) that converts a subscriber into a buyer. Once somebody has paid you anything, they're dramatically more likely to pay you again.

**Tripwire Funnel** — A funnel built around a tripwire offer at the front. Lead magnet to tripwire to upsells to main product.

## U

**Upsell** — An offer that fires after the first purchase. Not a second pitch, an upgrade or expansion of the decision the buyer just made.

**USP (Unique Selling Proposition)** — The specific thing that makes you different from everyone else doing what you do. Not "high quality." That's not a USP, that's table stakes.

## V

**Value-Based Pricing** — Pricing based on what the result is worth to the customer, not on what it costs you to deliver. Almost always higher than cost-plus pricing. The number to test before you assume you need to go lower.

**Value Stack** — Listing everything included in your offer with a value assigned to each piece, building to a total that makes the asking price feel like a steal. Direct response staple.

**VIP** — Tag for your highest-value customers. Different communication, different offers, sometimes different prices.

**Voice** — How a writer sounds. The cadence, the word choice, the relationship with the reader. The thing AI struggles to replicate without proper training.

**Voice Training** — Giving the AI examples of your real writing so it can approximate how you sound. Iterative. Never perfect, but close enough to save real time.

## W

**Warm Traffic** — People who already know you. Your list, your audience, your repeat visitors. Converts at multiples of what cold traffic does.

**Webinar Funnel** — Live presentation followed by an offer. Best for products over $500 because the format gives you sixty to ninety minutes to build trust and explain the offer.

**Welcome Sequence** — The first emails somebody gets after joining your list. The most important emails you'll ever write. Open rates two to three times higher than ongoing emails. Don't waste them.

**Win-Back Sequence** — An email sequence aimed at customers who've gone quiet. Relationship repair, not a discount trigger. The coupon is the last move, not the first.

# Appendix A: The Complete Prompt Library

---

This appendix collects prompts for situations not covered in depth elsewhere in the book. Think of it as a lookup tool — organized by category, with notes on when and how to use each one.

## Customer Research Prompts

Beyond the avatar and market discovery prompts from Part Two, these prompts help you build ongoing customer intelligence as your business develops.

**✦ CUSTOMER LANGUAGE MINING PROMPT**

```
Below is verbatim language from my target customers – forum
posts, reviews, community discussions, emails I've received:
[PASTE THE RAW CUSTOMER LANGUAGE] Analyze this language and
extract: 1. THE EXACT PHRASES they use to describe their
problem – verbatim, not paraphrased

2. EMOTIONAL VOCABULARY – the words that carry the most
emotional weight, sorted by: frustration words, hope words,
identity words, fear words

3. THE STORY STRUCTURE – how they tell the story of their
problem: what triggers it, what they've tried, where they
want to end up

4. THE UNSPOKEN DESIRE – what are they really hoping for
beyond the stated fix? What transformation, at the level of
identity, are they seeking?

5. THE RED FLAGS – what marketing language, approaches, or
claims make them roll their eyes or distrust?

6. HEADLINE AND SUBJECT LINE CANDIDATES – 8 headline options
```

```
using ONLY the language I've provided. No marketing speak.
Their words, their voice.
```

**Note:** *Run this prompt after every significant round of customer research. The output should go directly into your copy — not paraphrased, but used verbatim. Your customers' own words in your marketing is the closest thing to a conversion guarantee that exists.*

### ✦ TESTIMONIAL MINING PROMPT

```
I have the following customer testimonials and feedback:
[PASTE ALL CUSTOMER TESTIMONIALS, REVIEWS, OR FEEDBACK]
Please analyze this feedback and: 1. IDENTIFY THE STRONGEST
5 TESTIMONIALS — rank them on specificity of result,
emotional impact, objection-handling value, and
believability. Explain your ranking. 2. IDENTIFY THE KEY
THEMES — what results or transformations come up most
frequently? What language do customers use to describe
success? 3. IDENTIFY THE HIDDEN TESTIMONIALS — are there
statements buried in longer feedback that, extracted and
formatted as standalone quotes, would be powerful? Extract
them. 4. IDENTIFY THE GAPS — what testimonials don't I have
yet that I should proactively gather? What objections remain
unaddressed? 5. WRITE FOLLOW-UP QUESTIONS — for my top 3
customers, what specific follow-up questions would generate
better testimonials from them? (Questions that would prompt
more specific, result-focused responses.)
```

**Note:** *Most businesses have more testimonial material than they realize, just not organized effectively. This prompt helps you surface and structure what you already have before you invest in gathering new social proof.*

## Content and Copy Prompts

### ✦ ABOUT PAGE PROMPT

```
Write my About page in my brand voice. Here is everything
relevant: MY STORY: [The real story — how you got into this,
what you've learned, what shaped you, what you care about
most]

MY CREDENTIALS: [Relevant experience, results, expertise —
```

be honest about what's real]

MY CUSTOMER: [Who they are, what they care about, what they're trying to accomplish]

BRAND VOICE: [Your voice description] The About page should accomplish four things:

1. Establish genuine credibility without bragging – the goal is trust, not impressive

2. Create real human connection – they're deciding whether to trust you, not just assessing your qualifications

3. Show that you understand them – not just your own story, but why your story is relevant to their situation

4. End with a clear invitation – where do they go from here? Write in my voice. Personal, specific, not corporate. This page is the handshake – the moment someone decides whether this is a person they want to have in their life.

**Note:** *The About page is frequently one of the highest-traffic pages on a website and one of the most neglected. People go there specifically to decide whether to trust you — give them a reason to.*

## ✦ OBJECTION HANDLER PROMPT

I need to handle the objections that are preventing my target customer from buying. Here is the context: OFFER: [What you're selling]

CUSTOMER: [Avatar description]

KNOWN OBJECTIONS: [Every objection you've heard or can anticipate] For each objection:

1. STATE IT in the customer's exact words – how they'd phrase it in their head

2. DIAGNOSE THE ROOT FEAR – what deeper fear or concern is driving the stated objection?

3. THE EMPATHETIC ACKNOWLEDGMENT – how do I validate the objection before addressing it?

4. THE RESPONSE – what fact, reframe, evidence, or perspective shift makes the objection lose its power?

5. THE COPY – write 2-3 sentences of actual sales copy that handles this objection naturally ALSO: What is the most common objection which NOT stated – the thing people are thinking but not saying? This hidden objection is often more powerful than the stated ones. Format the output so I can

```
use it directly in sales page copy.
```

**Note:** *The hidden objection question often surfaces the most important thing. 'Is this going to work for me specifically?' almost always exists in the background. 'Am I capable of implementing this?' is common in how-to products. Address the unstated fears and conversion rates improve significantly.*

## Strategic Business Prompts

### ✦ PARTNERSHIP OPPORTUNITY PROMPT

```
I want to find strategic partnership opportunities to grow my business. Context: MY BUSINESS: [What you do, who you serve, what makes you valuable]

MY ASSETS: [What do I have that would be valuable to a partner – audience, expertise, products, content, credibility, traffic?]

MY GOALS FROM PARTNERSHIPS: [New customers? Revenue share? Credibility? Reach?] the host-beneficiary concept: identify businesses that already have the audience I want, and find a way to create mutual value by bringing my offer to that audience. Please identify partnership opportunities: 1. HOST-BENEFICIARY CANDIDATES: What businesses serve my target customer with non-competing products or services? List 10 specific types of businesses. 2. ASSET MATCHING: For each candidate type, what do I have that would be valuable to them? Revenue share? Free access for their audience? Co-branded content? Something else? 3. TOP 3 PARTNERSHIP TYPES: Of all candidates, which 3 offer the best combination of audience quality, reachability, and mutual value? 4. OUTREACH EMAIL: For my #1 partnership candidate, write the outreach email. It should: get to the point immediately, make a clear case for why their audience benefits, explain the mutual upside, and make a specific ask. 5. AFFILIATE PROGRAM DESIGN: Should I build a formal affiliate or ambassador program? If yes: what commission structure makes sense? What type of partner would be most valuable? How do I recruit them?
```

**Note:** *Host-beneficiary partnerships are often the fastest path to growth for businesses with limited ad budgets. One good partnership with a complementary business that has a large, relevant audience can outperform months of paid advertising at a fraction of the cost.*

# Appendix: 50 Prompts — Quick Reference

---

This appendix is a quick-reference companion. Each prompt can be adapted for any capable AI assistant. Replace the bracketed sections with your specific business context before running.

## MARKET RESEARCH PROMPTS (1–10)

### 1. Initial Market Discovery

```
What are the 5 most underserved sub-niches within [BROAD
MARKET] where a new direct-to-consumer business could enter
with less than $10,000 startup capital? For each: the
specific customer, their core pain, demonstrated spending
behavior, and why the market is underserved right now.
```

### 2. Pain Point Deep Dive

```
I'm studying buyers in [MARKET]. What are the 10 most acute,
expensive, or emotionally significant problems they have
that existing products consistently fail to solve? Rank by
urgency and spending willingness. For each: describe it in
the customer's language, explain what makes it expensive or
emotionally significant, and describe what the best existing
solutions miss.
```

### 3. Amazon Review Mining

```
Below are 1-3 star reviews from [PRODUCT CATEGORY] products
on Amazon: [PASTE REVIEWS]. Analyze these and identify: the
most common unsolved problems, the exact phrases customers
use to describe their frustration, what an ideal product
would need to deliver to earn 5 stars from these customers,
and the opportunity this creates for a new entrant.
```

### 4. Reddit Research Synthesis

Below are posts and comments from [SPECIFIC SUBREDDIT(S)]: [PASTE CONTENT]. Synthesize this into: the 5 most recurring themes and problems, the specific language used to describe the problems, what the community has tried and found lacking, and the most frequently desired but unfulfilled solution.

### 5. Search Intent Analysis

Someone searching [SPECIFIC SEARCH QUERY] — what is their likely situation? What problem are they trying to solve? How aware are they of solutions? What objections will they carry into their research? What would need to happen for them to buy from a brand they've never heard of? Design the ideal first page they should land on.

### 6. Trend Analysis

What are the major macro trends affecting [MARKET] over the next 3-5 years? For each trend: what's driving it, who it affects most, how fast it's moving, and what opportunity or threat it creates for a new entrant. Which trends create windows that will close, and which create durable tailwinds?

### 7. Buyer Segmentation

Within the market for [PRODUCT CATEGORY], identify 4 meaningfully different buyer segments. For each: demographic and psychographic profile, their specific version of the core problem, what they've already tried, what they're willing to pay, and what marketing message would resonate most strongly.

### 8. Market Validation Questions

I'm considering entering the [MARKET] with [PRODUCT CONCEPT]. What are the 10 most important questions I need to answer before committing to this market? For each question: why it matters, what the answer would tell me, and how I'd go about finding the answer with limited resources.

### 9. Competitive Gap Finder

```
Based on this competitive landscape research: [PASTE
RESEARCH], identify the top 5 gaps – unmet needs or
underserved segments – that none of the existing players are
specifically designed for. For each gap: describe it,
explain why existing players don't fill it, and assess
whether a new entrant could fill it sustainably.
```

### 10. Customer Language Extraction

```
Below is raw customer language from [MARKET] – forum posts,
reviews, comments: [PASTE CONTENT]. Extract: the verbatim
phrases they use to describe their problem, the emotional
vocabulary (frustration words, hope words, identity words),
the story structure (trigger → failed attempts → desired
outcome), and 5 headline candidates using only their own
language.
```

## STRATEGY PROMPTS (11–20)

### 11. Three Levers Audit

```
Apply the three-lever framework to my business: [DESCRIBE
YOUR BUSINESS – what you sell, who to, what it costs,
current revenue]. For each lever – more customers, higher
transaction value, more frequent purchase – identify the
single highest-leverage improvement I could make in the next
90 days with limited budget. Give me the sequencing: what to
do first, second, third, and why.
```

### 12. Preeminence Positioning

```
Apply the Strategy of Preeminence to my business: [DESCRIBE
YOUR BUSINESS AND CUSTOMER]. How would a business operating
from genuine preeminence – acting as trusted advisor, not
vendor – communicate differently? What would change about my
offers, my copy, my email sequence, and my customer service
model?
```

### 13. Customer Lifetime Value Modeling

```
Model the customer lifetime value for my business: [DESCRIBE
YOUR BUSINESS, PRODUCTS, PRICES, ESTIMATED REPEAT PURCHASE
```

```
RATE]. Show LTV at 12 months, 24 months, and 36 months. Then
show me: how does LTV change if repeat purchase rate
improves by 20%? By 40%? What's the maximum I can afford to
spend on customer acquisition at current LTV?
```

## 14. USP Stress Test

```
Here is my current USP/positioning statement: [PASTE IT].
Stress test it: Can any competitor make this exact claim? Is
it specific enough that it would rule out customers who
aren't right for me? Does it make a promise the target
customer specifically wants? What would need to change to
make this positioning defensible and differentiating?
```

## 15. Risk Reversal Design

```
Design the strongest, most credible risk reversal for my
offer: [DESCRIBE OFFER AND PRICE]. What guarantee would make
a skeptical, once-burned prospect feel that buying is less
risky than not buying? How do I word it so it's compelling
without being unenforceable? What are the conditions that
make this guarantee sustainable for my business?
```

## 16. Host-Beneficiary Partnerships

```
For my business serving [CUSTOMER AVATAR], identify 10 non-
competing businesses that serve the same customer and would
be logical host-beneficiary partners. For the top 3:
describe the exact partnership structure that works for both
parties, what I bring to them, what they bring to me, and
how I'd approach the conversation.
```

## 17. Revenue Model Stress Test

```
Here is my business model: [DESCRIBE IT — products, prices,
customer acquisition plan, expected volumes]. Build a
conservative, base, and optimistic case for 12-month
revenue. Identify: where does this model break down if
volume is 50% lower than base? What single unit-economics
change would have the biggest positive impact? What is the
most dangerous assumption I'm making?
```

## 18. Pre-Mortem Analysis

```
I'm planning to [DESCRIBE PLAN]. Assume it fails badly in 12
months. From that vantage point, list the 10 most plausible
```

```
reasons it failed. For each: the early warning sign I should
watch for, the point at which it could have been corrected,
and what I'd do differently if I'd anticipated it. Rank by
likelihood and severity.
```

### 19. Competitive Response Planning

```
If I enter [MARKET] and start gaining traction with
[POSITIONING], what is the most dangerous competitive
response from the dominant players? What are they most
likely to do, and when? How do I build in structural
advantages and customer loyalty that make their response
less effective?
```

### 20. Bottleneck Identification

```
Here is my funnel data: [PASTE CONVERSION RATES AT EACH
STEP]. Where is the biggest bottleneck — the step where the
most improvement is available for the least effort? What
would a 20% improvement at that specific bottleneck do to my
overall revenue? What are the 3 most likely causes of the
underperformance at that step?
```

## OFFER AND PRICING PROMPTS (21–30)

### 21. Value Stack Designer

```
My core offer is [DESCRIBE OFFER] at [$PRICE]. Design a
bonus stack of 5 items that: directly addresses my
customer's top objections, has high perceived value and low
delivery cost, and logically complements the core offer. For
each bonus: name it, describe it, assign a legitimate value,
explain which specific objection or desire it addresses.
```

### 22. Offer Naming Generator

```
My offer is [DESCRIBE IT GENERICALLY]. Generate 10 name
options that: use my customer's language rather than
marketing language, describe the transformation rather than
the product, are specific enough to be memorable, and would
make my ideal customer think 'that's exactly what I need.'
Rank them and explain the top 3.
```

## 23. Upsell Sequence Design

A customer just purchased [INITIAL PRODUCT] at [$PRICE]. Design a two-step upsell sequence: (1) an order bump on the checkout page and (2) a one-click upsell immediately after payment. For each: the product, the price, the headline, the core argument for why they should add it right now, and the expected take rate with reasoning.

## 24. Pricing Architecture Design

Design a three-tier pricing structure for [BUSINESS TYPE] serving [CUSTOMER]. Entry tier: low friction first-purchase option. Core tier: where most customers should land. Premium tier: maximum support and access. For each tier: what's included, what's the price, and what's the core reason someone would choose this tier over the others.

## 25. Guarantee Language Generator

Write 5 variations of my guarantee for [OFFER]: from a basic 30-day money-back to a bold results-based guarantee. For each: the exact wording, the conditions, the strength level (bold/moderate/conservative), and the expected impact on conversion rate. Tell me which guarantee my most skeptical customer would most believe.

## 26. Free Plus Shipping Product Finder

For a business selling [MAIN PRODUCTS] to [CUSTOMER AVATAR], identify the ideal free plus shipping product. It should: be exciting to my avatar, be small and light (low shipping cost), cost under $5-6 to produce or source, and naturally create desire for my main product. Give 3 candidates with production notes and economics.

## 27. Tripwire Offer Design

Design a tripwire offer for my business. Core product: [DESCRIBE IT]. The tripwire should: be valuable on its own, be priced at $7-37, be an obvious natural precursor to the main offer, and feel like a deal so good the customer would feel foolish not taking it. Describe the product, the price, the framing, and the transition to the main offer.

### 28. Bundle Creation

What product bundles make sense for my business selling [LIST OF PRODUCTS]? For each bundle candidate: what products are included, what is the bundle price (vs. individual prices), what is the psychological appeal to my customer, and what is the revenue impact per customer if X% choose the bundle over individual items?

### 29. Launch Pricing Strategy

I'm launching [OFFER] for the first time. What is the optimal launch pricing strategy? Should I use introductory pricing, full price from day one, or a price-increase structure? What are the long-term positioning implications of each approach? What's the recommended approach for my specific market and offer?

### 30. Irresistibility Audit

Here is my complete offer: [DESCRIBE EVERYTHING – core product, bonuses, price, guarantee, urgency]. Reading this as my most skeptical ideal customer: does this offer feel irresistible? What's the weakest element? What would need to change for a qualified but hesitant buyer to feel that saying no is the riskier choice? Be specific.

## COPYWRITING PROMPTS (31–40)

### 31. Headline Generator

Write 15 headline variations for [OFFER/PAGE/EMAIL]. Cover these angles: specific transformation, time to result, pain being solved, objection being overcome, social proof, how-to, curiosity hook, identity/belonging, fear of missing out, and bold promise. Rate the top 5 on specificity, emotional resonance, and believability.

### 32. Opening Hook Library

Write 8 different opening hooks for [COPY TYPE] about [TOPIC] targeting [AVATAR]. Each should use a different approach: origin story, provocative statement, unexpected analogy, startling statistic, common misconception, universal experience, bold promise, or problem statement. Each hook should make the reader want the second sentence.

## 33. Brand Story Development

Here are the raw facts of my story: [SHARE YOUR REAL STORY]. Help me craft this into a compelling brand story with: the hero's journey structure, the universal theme that makes it relatable beyond my specific experience, a 150-word version for my About page, a 400-word version for email, and the one-sentence core premise that drives everything I do.

## 34. Testimonial Request Templates

Write 3 testimonial request email templates that would prompt specific, result-focused responses from customers. Each template should guide the customer to describe: their situation before, the specific result they achieved, one concrete detail that makes it credible, and what they'd tell a friend considering the product. Make them easy to respond to without sounding like a form.

## 35. FAQ Section Writer

Write a complete FAQ section for [OFFER]. Identify the 12 most important questions my customer would ask before buying – including the uncomfortable ones – and write honest, specific, persuasive answers. Include questions about results, timeline, difficulty, support, payment, refunds, and 'is this right for me.'

## 36. Social Media Content Batch

Write 10 social media posts for [PLATFORM] promoting [OFFER/BRAND/TOPIC]. Mix of content types: educational (3), story (2), social proof (2), promotional (2), engagement question (1). For each: the post itself, relevant hashtags if applicable, and the specific goal of the post (awareness, click, engagement, conversion).

## 37. Content Calendar Design

Build a 90-day content calendar for my business. Context: [AUDIENCE, CHANNELS, PUBLISHING CAPACITY, CURRENT GOALS].

```
Identify: 6 core content themes, the weekly publishing
cadence by channel, how content builds across the period,
where promotional content fits, and which 5 pieces should be
treated as evergreen investments.
```

### 38. PS and Postscript Lines

```
Write 10 P.S. options for [EMAIL TYPE AND CONTEXT]. Each
P.S. should serve a specific function: add urgency, reveal a
bonus, handle a specific objection, add social proof, add a
personal touch, create curiosity, or reinforce the main CTA.
Make each one feel natural and not tacked on.
```

### 39. Devil's Advocate Review

```
Here is my [SALES PAGE / EMAIL / LANDING PAGE]: [PASTE
CONTENT]. As the most skeptical version of my target
customer, tell me the 10 things that would prevent you from
buying. Be specific about: unsubstantiated claims, missing
information, trust gaps, weak points in the value
proposition, and the one change most likely to move the
needle.
```

### 40. Simplification Pass

```
Here is a piece of copy: [PASTE COPY]. Edit it for clarity
and simplicity without losing persuasive substance. Shorten
sentences over 20 words. Replace jargon with plain language.
Cut anything that doesn't earn its place. The goal: an
intelligent person should be able to read this once and
understand everything, with no need to reread.
```

## EMAIL MARKETING PROMPTS (41–50)

### 41. Cart Abandonment Sequence

```
Write a 3-email cart abandonment sequence for someone who
added [PRODUCT] to their cart but didn't complete purchase.
Email 1 (1 hour after): friendly reminder with the most
likely objection addressed. Email 2 (24 hours): tackle a
different objection or add a bonus. Email 3 (48 hours):
final reminder with any real urgency. Write all 3 in full,
```

in voice: [DESCRIBE].

## 42. Re-engagement Campaign

Write a 3-email re-engagement campaign for subscribers inactive for 90+ days. Goal: re-engage the engageable, gracefully release the rest. Email 1: honest reach-out with something valuable. Email 2: ask directly if they still want to hear from you, with a clear keep-me/remove-me choice. Email 3: final notice before cleaning the list. Avoid guilt and manipulation throughout.

## 43. Win-Back Sequence

Write a 3-email win-back sequence for customers who bought once but haven't purchased in 12+ months. Voice: [DESCRIBE]. The sequence should: acknowledge the gap honestly without guilt, offer something new or relevant, make an exclusive returnee offer, and keep the relationship warm even if they don't buy again.

## 44. Post-Purchase Nurture Email 1

Write the first post-purchase email for a customer who just bought [SPECIFIC PRODUCT]. This email arrives within 1 hour of purchase. Its purpose: confirm they made a great decision, tell them specifically what to expect and when, give them one immediately actionable thing related to the product, and set up the next email. Voice: [DESCRIBE]. Do NOT include any additional purchase recommendations in this email.

## 45. Referral Program Announcement Email

Write an email announcing my referral/ambassador program to my existing customer list. Voice: [DESCRIBE]. The email should: explain what the program is in plain language, make the benefits feel exciting, explain exactly how to join, and convey authentic enthusiasm without feeling like a recruitment pitch. Include subject line options.

## 46. Holiday/Seasonal Campaign

Write a [HOLIDAY/SEASON] promotional email campaign (3 emails) for my business. Context: [DESCRIBE BUSINESS, OFFER, AUDIENCE]. The campaign should: connect the holiday/season authentically to my brand and customer (not forced), present a compelling seasonal offer, and maintain my brand voice throughout. Include subject lines and full email copy for all 3.

## 47. New Subscriber Conversion Email

Write an email for new subscribers who have been on my list for 30 days but haven't made a purchase. Context: [DESCRIBE BUSINESS AND OFFER]. This email should: acknowledge they've been getting my emails, make the softest possible first offer, and focus on whether this product is right for them (not just selling it to them). Voice: [DESCRIBE].

## 48. Flash Sale Announcement

Write a flash sale email for [PRODUCT] at [DISCOUNT] for [TIME PERIOD]. Voice: [DESCRIBE]. The email should: open with a hook that isn't just 'SALE!', give a credible and honest reason for the sale, create urgency that's real rather than manufactured, and include a clear subject line and CTA. Also write a follow-up reminder email for Day 2 of the sale.

## 49. Event/Webinar Invitation

Write an invitation email for [EVENT/WEBINAR NAME AND TOPIC]. Context: [DESCRIBE THE EVENT, DATE, TIME, WHAT PEOPLE WILL LEARN, WHY THEY SHOULD ATTEND]. Voice: [DESCRIBE]. The email should make attendance feel worthwhile — lead with what they'll get, not what I'm offering. Include 2 subject line options and a follow-up reminder for registered attendees.

## 50. The Jay the framework Full Business Audit

Conduct a complete strategic audit of my business using these frameworks. My business in full: [DESCRIBE COMPLETELY — what you sell, who you sell to, pricing, current revenue, list size, main funnel, customer acquisition costs, repeat purchase rate, current positioning]. Apply: Strategy of Preeminence (am I positioned as trusted advisor?), three levers (which am I underutilizing most?), host-beneficiary opportunities (what partnerships am I leaving on the table?), risk reversal (how can I take more risk off my buyer?), and lifetime value optimization (am I maximizing each customer relationship?). Give me the three highest-leverage changes I could make in the next 90 days, with

```
specific implementation steps for each.
```

# Notes

---

The following notes identify the sources for specific factual claims made in the text. Software pricing, platform statistics, and benchmark figures should be verified at time of use — these were accurate at time of writing and will change.

**WordPress market share**

WordPress powers approximately 43 percent of all websites globally as of April 2026. Source: W3Techs Web Technology Surveys, w3techs.com/technologies/details/cm-wordpress. Updated continuously; verify for current figure.

**Email marketing ROI**

The $36–$42 return per dollar spent in email marketing is drawn from the Litmus 2023 State of Email report and the Data & Marketing Association's response rate reports. Figures vary by industry and list quality. Both reports are available at litmus.com and thedma.org respectively.

**Customer acquisition cost: new vs. existing customers**

The five-to-seven times cost differential between acquiring new customers versus selling to existing ones is a widely cited figure in marketing literature, most associated with research from Bain & Company and Frederick Reichheld's work on customer loyalty. The precise ratio varies significantly by industry. Source: Reichheld, F.F. and Sasser, W.E., 'Zero defections: quality comes to services,' Harvard Business Review, September–October 1990.

### Funnel conversion benchmarks

Landing page conversion rates, order bump take rates, and upsell acceptance rates cited throughout Part Four are directional ranges drawn from industry data published by FunnelKit (funnelkit.com), ClickFunnels, and direct response practitioners across multiple business types. These are heuristic ranges — actual results vary substantially based on offer type, price point, traffic source, and copy quality.

### Cart abandonment rate

The claim that checkout abandonment is a significant conversion problem is supported by research from the Baymard Institute (baymard.com), which tracks checkout usability across major e-commerce sites and publishes annual abandonment rate data. As of 2024, the average documented cart abandonment rate across e-commerce was approximately 70 percent.

### Claude pricing

Claude Pro is priced at $20 per month as of April 2026. Anthropic offers additional plan tiers including Max ($100–$200/month) and Team plans. Pricing is subject to change. Verify current plans at claude.ai/pricing.

#### FunnelKit pricing

FunnelKit Funnel Builder Pro starts at $99.50 per year; FunnelKit Automations Pro starts at $249 per year as of April 2026. Verify current pricing at funnelkit.com.

#### ClickFunnels pricing

ClickFunnels Launch plan is priced at $97 per month as of April 2026, with annual billing discounts available. Verify current pricing at clickfunnels.com.

#### Direct response marketing foundations

The core principles of measurable, results-accountable advertising described throughout this book draw from a tradition that includes Claude Hopkins, Scientific Advertising (1923); David Ogilvy, Ogilvy on Advertising (1983); and Eugene Schwartz, Breakthrough Advertising (1966). All three remain in print and are considered foundational texts in the field.

#### The three business growth levers

The three-lever framework — more customers, higher transaction value, more frequent purchase — is a foundational concept in direct response marketing. the book Getting Everything You Can Out of All You've Got (2000, St. Martin's Press) provides an extended treatment. The mathematical observation that modest improvements across all three levers produce geometric revenue growth is the central strategic argument of Part Three of this book.

#### The Attractive Character / Hero brand persona

The Hero framework in Chapter 10 builds on Russell Brunson's concept of the Attractive Character, developed in Expert Secrets (2017, Morgan James Publishing). Brunson's framework is the clearest early articulation of why a consistent human personality at the center of a direct-to-consumer business outperforms faceless brand communication.

#### Value equation for offer design

The offer design framework in Chapter 18 — centering on dream outcome, perceived likelihood, time delay, and effort required — draws from Alex Hormozi, $100M Offers (2021, Acquisition.com). Hormozi's treatment of offer construction is the most practically useful modern text on the subject.

# Sources and Further Reading

---

The following notes identify the source material, framework origins, and further reading for the key ideas in this book. All software pricing cited should be verified directly with vendors before purchase — pricing changes frequently and this information was accurate at time of writing but will not remain so indefinitely.

### On Direct Response Marketing — Foundational Works

Claude Hopkins, Scientific Advertising (1923). The foundational text on measurable, results-accountable advertising. Hopkins' insistence that advertising should be treated as a science — with testable hypotheses and tracked outcomes — remains the most important principle in direct response.

David Ogilvy, Ogilvy on Advertising (1983). The practitioner's companion to Hopkins, integrating brand thinking with direct response discipline. Ogilvy's chapter on what works in advertising remains accurate forty years later.

Eugene Schwartz, Breakthrough Advertising (1966, reprinted 2004). The most technically sophisticated book ever written on copywriting, specifically around matching copy to the awareness level of the prospect. Schwartz's five stages of market awareness are the framework behind many of the avatar and copy prompts in this book.

Gary Halbert, The Boron Letters (2013). Written as letters from prison to his son, the most accessible introduction to direct response thinking available. Halbert's voice — casual, specific, relentlessly practical — influenced the tone of this book more than he would know.

## On Offer Design and Business Strategy

Russell Brunson, Expert Secrets (2017). The source of the Attractive Character framework, which this book's Hero chapter extends and reframes for AI-assisted content production. Brunson's three-part business model (attract, ascend, convert) is foundational to the funnel architecture described in Part Four.

Russell Brunson, DotCom Secrets (2015). The most practical book on funnel architecture available. The value ladder concept directly underlies the order bump and upsell structure described in Chapter 14.

Alex Hormozi, $100M Offers (2021). The best modern treatment of offer design. Hormozi's value equation — dream outcome, perceived likelihood, time delay, effort required — is the framework behind the irresistible offer prompts in Part Six.

## On the Three Business Growth Levers

The three-lever framework (more customers, higher transaction value, more frequent purchase) is a foundational concept in direct response marketing and business optimization with roots in the work of multiple practitioners. Jay the framework, a marketing strategist who has written and taught extensively on business growth, popularized a version of this framework under the name 'three ways to grow a business.' His book Getting Everything You Can Out of All You've Got (2000) is the primary source for readers who want to explore this thinking in depth. The core mathematical insight — that small improvements compounding across all three levers produce geometric revenue growth — is the central strategic argument of Part Three.

## On AI Tools Referenced in This Book

Claude, produced by Anthropic. Current pricing and plan information: claude.ai/pricing. The Pro plan referenced throughout this book is $20 per month at time of writing. Anthropic's pricing structure, plan names, and feature sets have evolved and will continue to evolve — verify current information directly.

ChatGPT, produced by OpenAI: openai.com. A capable alternative to Claude for the prompting workflows described in this book.

Gemini, produced by Google: gemini.google.com. Another capable alternative with strong performance on research and synthesis tasks.

### On Funnel and Marketing Software Referenced in This Book

FunnelKit Funnel Builder Pro and FunnelKit Automations Pro: funnelkit.com. Current pricing: Funnel Builder Pro starts at $99.50/year; Automations Pro starts at $249/year. Verify at funnelkit.com.

ClickFunnels: clickfunnels.com. Current entry plan at $97/month. A capable alternative to FunnelKit for businesses not on WordPress.

WordPress: wordpress.org. Powers approximately 43 percent of all websites globally as of April 2026, per W3Techs (w3techs.com/technologies/details/cm-wordpress).

WooCommerce: woocommerce.com. The e-commerce layer used throughout the stack described in Chapter 3.

SiteGround: siteground.com. The hosting provider referenced in Chapter 3. Pricing varies by plan and promotional period — verify current rates directly.

### On Email Marketing Performance Benchmarks

Email open rates, click rates, and conversion benchmarks cited in Part Five are directional ranges drawn from industry reporting by Mailchimp, Klaviyo, and Campaign Monitor, cross-referenced against the author's direct experience across multiple categories. These figures vary significantly by industry, list quality, sender reputation, and subject line — treat them as orientation, not targets. Current benchmark reports are published annually by all three platforms at no cost.

### On Funnel Conversion Benchmarks

Landing page conversion rates, order bump take rates, and upsell acceptance rates cited in Parts Four and Six are drawn from ranges commonly reported by FunnelKit, ClickFunnels, and direct response practitioners across a variety of business types. These are heuristic ranges — actual results vary substantially based on offer type, price point, traffic source, and copy quality. They should be treated as starting assumptions to test against, not performance standards.

# About the Author

---

Brian Kasday has spent four decades in direct response advertising — the branch of marketing where every dollar spent is tracked, every result is measured, and there is nowhere to hide when something doesn't work.

Over that career, he has helped generate hundreds of millions of dollars in measurable sales across categories including cellular communications, satellite television, merchandise, and financial services. He has written and overseen copy across television, radio, print, direct mail, and digital — in each case tracking what works and what doesn't across formats, audiences, and economic conditions spanning four decades of change.

Unlike most marketing books, which are written by people who teach marketing, this one was written by someone who spent his entire career doing it. The difference shows up in the specifics: the offer structures that close, the copy patterns that hold up under the pressure of real campaigns, the email disciplines that build real customer relationships over time. These are not frameworks assembled from other people's observations. They are conclusions earned from running real campaigns and watching them succeed or fail.

When large language model AI tools began reaching genuine capability, Kasday approached them the way he has approached every new channel in forty years: with skepticism about the hype, direct testing of the actual results, and a focus on whether the tool could perform against the principles that drive direct response. The answer he found, with the right approach, was yes.

This book is the distillation of that experience — forty years of direct response discipline, amplified by AI, and systematized into a framework that works. You now have access to the same strategic thinking and tactical execution that previously required decades to master. The only question remaining is what you'll build with it.

— — —

## Before you put this book down

The 50 prompts in the back of this book are free in copy-and-paste format — go to mmsvegas.com/resources, enter your email, and they'll land in your inbox ready to drop straight into your AI of choice.

mmsvegas.com/resources

One more thing, and it matters more than you'd think for a book like this one: if it earned its keep, leave an honest review at mmsvegas.com/marketing-review. It takes two minutes, and reviews are how independent books get found.

www.ingramcontent.com/pod-product-compliance
Lightning Source LLC
LaVergne TN
LVHW010642110826
845149LV00014B/2925

* 9 7 9 8 9 9 6 1 2 6 4 0 8 *